Called to Freedom

D1572141

Called to Freedom

Why You Can Be Christian and Libertarian

Edited by
ELISE DANIEL

Foreword by
NORMAN HORN

WIPF & STOCK · Eugene, Oregon

CALLED TO FREEDOM
Why You Can Be Christian and Libertarian

Wipf & Stock
An Imprint of Wipf and Stock Publishers
199 W. 8th Ave., Suite 3
Eugene, OR 97401

www.wipfandstock.com

PAPERBACK ISBN: 978-1-4982-8094-5
HARDCOVER ISBN: 978-1-4982-8096-9
EBOOK ISBN: 978-1-4982-8095-2

Manufactured in the U.S.A.   JANUARY 20, 2017

To our spouses, Rachel Barkley, Kristopher Daniel, Jason Isaacs, Kira Luca, and Leah and Jason Hughey to each other. Thank you for supporting us on this journey. We also dedicate this book to anyone who is working to reconcile Christianity with libertarianism.

"What God does is well done. Do not claim to know more than He. God has given organs to this frail creature; let them develop and grow strong by exercise, use, experience, and liberty."

—FREDERIC BASTIAT, THE LAW

Contents

Contributors

Elise Daniel is a writer and communications professional in Washington, DC. She graduated from James Madison University with a BBA in economics.

Jacqueline Isaacs is the inaugural Fellow in Strategic Communication at the American Studies Program in Washington, DC. She earned her MBA in marketing at Johns Hopkins University and her BS in government at Oral Roberts University.

Jason Hughey is a certified personal trainer and group fitness instructor. He earned his BA in government from Regent University in 2012 and worked for several liberty-advancing nonprofits before switching to the fitness industry full-time.

Taylor Barkley lives in Washington, DC with his wife and works at a public policy organization and part-time with Search Ministries. He graduated from Taylor University with a degree in history and political science.

Leah Hughey is a graduate of Regent University, where she studied government and history. She works at a Christian ministry focused on fostering collaboration between charities and churches to solve social problems in the cities they serve. Leah has been happily married to coauthor Jason since 2013.

Philip Luca is an award-winning marketing strategist working with tech companies and startups in the DC area. He currently serves on the board of the American Marketing Association, DC as the VP of Social Media. He holds two graduate degrees from Liberty University in digital media and theology.

Foreword

Dr. Norman Horn

We live in strange times. The Christian right in America is struggling to find its identity now that its dominance in the GOP is waning. The Christian left appears to be having a field day with the advent of its favored social programs such as the Affordable Care Act. Yet the left repeatedly faces contradictions with core Christian values as the state ratchets up its power following every bit of ground it gains. Some Christians feel caught in that murky middle, not knowing exactly how to either engage with or retract from the surrounding chaotic elements of our culture. The confusion in how to deal with the state is palpable.

Denying the encroachment of the state is becoming increasingly difficult anywhere you look. Interventionism and wars are the normative measures of foreign affairs, and America's already gargantuan military has become even more expensive than ever before. Worse still are the results: "blowback" from interventions in the Middle East becomes more evident day by day as the refugee crisis continues and violence escalates around the world. We more frequently see examples of police violence as well as violence against police. Citizen confidence in law enforcement is at its lowest point in years. The War on Drugs continues but never seems to solve real drug problems in communities. Taxation goes up as spending, and social programs spin out of control. Regulations are unpredictable and burdensome, slowing economic expansion in many industries. Whereas the government once codified certain social mores in law, the same government now presses individuals and businesses to service those with whom they disagree. Power wielded unjustly in one way can just as easily be wielded unjustly the other way around.

At the same time, interest in libertarianism has grown as the state continues consolidating power. Christians relatively ignored libertarianism in the twentieth century, not for lack of libertarian Christian voices altogether but for the overwhelming volume of the non-libertarian voices. Rejecting the teachings of the religious right in favor of libertarianism was completely anathema to most Christians until recently. Moreover, the specter of Ayn Rand loomed over the libertarian movement. Her strident atheism was frequently associated with libertarians, despite the fact Rand personally opposed libertarianism.

The so-called "libertarian moment" may or may not be upon us now, depending on who you ask, but we are certainly seeing a renewed interest in libertarian ideas in the church at large. Libertarianism is openly debated on Christian radio, mentioned in Christian publications, and considered a realistic alternative to the left-right debate. Despite this uptick of general interest, Christians have always involved themselves in the progress of liberty and in the development of libertarian ideas. Whether we consider the Levellers, many of America's founding fathers, William Wilberforce's campaign to end slavery in England, or the genesis of many libertarian institutions in the twentieth century, Christianity has been an important motivating factor for building a free society.

Truly, life-long Christian and consistent libertarian thinker Dr. Ron Paul has helped bring libertarianism into the forefront of political conversation with his 2008 and 2012 presidential campaigns, and his example continues to inspire Christians to think differently. But the battle is not even close to won, and Christians in particular must return with vigor to a passion for true liberty.

The problem, in many respects, is the lack of synthesis of coherent biblical theology with sound economics and political theory. Theologians often lack knowledge of economics and political science and thereby make errors of thought and judgment that lead them astray about the nature of the state, sound economic policy, and civil liberties. It is relatively easy to find decent ministers and theologians who erroneously think that socialism is justified in the Bible. It is far more difficult to find those who can explain the fantastic benefits of free markets. Libertarians who claim Christ, on the other hand, often do not feel confident expressing the theological underpinnings of a philosophy of liberty. An interpretation of Romans

13 that does not tacitly justify all government actions, for instance, is not something you typically learn in Sunday school.

What shall we do then? The answer, as you might expect, is to heed the apostle Paul's call in Romans 12:2 to "renew our minds," attending to both scripture and evident reason to understand how the world works and to realize that liberty is key toward a peaceful and prosperous world.

Some Christians object that libertarian Christians are attempting to justify a human philosophy with scripture as intellectual cover. This criticism, however, could not be more wrong. Christians are now recognizing that *politically* conservative ideas do not match up well with *theologically* conservative principles. The state neither works effectively to build a free society nor promotes Christian witness and character. Thus, libertarian Christians are not inventing new theology or twisting the words of scripture but rather are recapturing the sacredness of the kingdom of God in a spiritual battle against the kingdoms of this world. This isn't a new idea; it's ancient. *We are now in a renaissance of libertarian Christian ideas, and it is being led by young voices drawing upon the wisdom of old voices.*

This book you hold in your hands (or read by the backlight of your Kindle or mobile device) is a testament to that leadership. Elise Daniel kicks it off by talking about the political tension among Christians today. Jacqueline Isaacs addresses the basic question of compatibility between libertarianism and Christianity. Jason Hughey surveys what the Bible says about the state. Taylor Barkley describes the danger of forcing the entirety of Christian moral codes in law. Leah Hughey reminds us that free markets and property rights bring peace and prosperity in a manner consistent with Christian practice. Philip Luca concludes with a passionate argument for liberty by describing the spiritual and economic poverty of post-Soviet Romania. All of these voices have demonstrated their commitment to Christ first, and that commitment inspires them to teach others about the virtues of libertarian ideas.

We can be very hopeful for the future despite the evils of the state. Poverty is declining due to the bounty of the market. Antipathy toward the state and its abuses are on the rise. And of course, the freedom all Christians have *in Christ* brings certainty and full hope that our future is secure. It is, in fact, that security and hope that drives us to promote liberty in the first place. We can herald a new age that displaces the state and builds a freer, more peaceful, more prosperous world, not won with violence but with love, service, and respect for all.

Might libertarianism actually be the most consistent political position for a Christian? Read on and find out for yourself.

Acknowledgments

We would like to thank Elizabeth Anderson, Gregory Ayers, Jonathon Bair, Lindsey Grudnicki, Amber Joyce, Kelly Miller, and Laurie Stiles for thoroughly editing our work and helping us further improve the content of this book. We are privileged to have worked with each of you and credit your sharp minds for helping develop this project to completion.

Introduction
Elise Daniel

I rolled my suitcase across the red brick campus at Wake Forest University, gazing up at the white rotunda. The air was heavy with humidity and thick with the enthusiasm of students traveling from across the globe to share a new experience together.

A young woman greeted me in the lobby of Polo Hall and handed me a schedule. This was where sixty other students and I would spend the next week of our summers: at a libertarian seminar with back-to-back lectures and discussion groups on topics covering liberty, economics, and morality. I reminded myself the weeklong summer sacrifice would be worth the impressive addition to my resume. What I did not expect was that it would become one of the most intellectually formative weeks of my education.

I grew up in a conservative, Christian home with a marine father and Texas roots. I was a Republican long before I was old enough to vote. When I was in middle school, I defended George W. Bush against attacks from my peers and sometimes even my teachers. In high school, I phone banked for my Republican congressman's campaign and stuck his reelection signs in the county parkway medians. In college, I frequented College Republican meetings on Wednesday nights and looked forward to the Conservative Political Action Conference (CPAC) that I attended with them in DC. My college roommate and I still laugh about my reaction to the 2008 presidential election. After the final results rolled in, I sobbed facedown in my pillow, despairing over our nation's future under President Barack Obama's leadership. I was slightly joking—but not completely.

1

Six months later, I channeled my Obama trauma into a summer internship application with a grassroots organization dedicated to fighting his anti-freedom policies. During my time there, the interns were required to read works by philosophers and economists like Friedrich Hayek and Milton Friedman. Influenced by these thinkers, many of my coworkers called themselves libertarians. They challenged my neo-conservative views and introduced me to *libertarianism*, a political philosophy that holds liberty as its principal objective.[1]

As a conservative, I always believed in freedom. But I began to wonder, do Republicans *always* stand for freedom? Or do libertarians carry this objective out more honestly and consistently in practice than conservatives? Though I remained firm in my Christian faith, I became politically curious.

When I told my parents I signed up for a libertarian seminar, they looked at me as if I had just told them I was going to Burning Man. Because God ordained government in the Bible[2] and Christ said, "Render to Caesar the things that are Caesar's,"[3] they believe it is very difficult to reconcile libertarianism with Christianity (Jason Hughey will examine these verses in depth in chapter 2).

I imagine my parents view libertarians as anarchist pagans who are primarily focused on legalizing drugs and living without any moral restraints, because that is how I once perceived them. While I no longer likened libertarians to pagans, I had no idea I was entering a community that seemed so godless.

After the seminar lectures at Wake Forest, we broke into groups to discuss and debate the merits of great thinkers like Adam Smith and Ludwig Von Mises. Much of the discussion moved from questions of economic policy to philosophical questions of morality and human nature.

In one group, we discussed the morality of the law. The leader of the group asked us a question about self-ownership: "Who owns you—the government or yourself?" The question struck me as odd. As a Christian, I did not believe that I was the owner of myself, because I did not create me, God created me. Though God gives us a level of autonomy and will hold us accountable for our actions, Paul writes to the Corinthians that we are not our own; we were bought at a high price when Christ redeemed our lives

---

1. Boaz, "Libertarianism."
2. Rom 13:1
3. Mark 12:17

on the cross.[4] As a conservative and a Christian, I did not believe the state owned me either.

With some hesitation, I challenged the group. "Christians, for example, might say God owns you," I added. I scanned the circle, meeting stoic faces in polite disagreement along the way. After a long pause, the discussion leader responded, "Yes, that's one view." The girl next to me followed up, arguing why self-ownership is the only logical answer. The group nodded. Maybe I was the only one in the group who believed in God.

The next group discussion focused on Ayn Rand, author of *Atlas Shrugged* and *The Virtue of Selfishness*. Rand upholds selfishness as a virtue and sacrifice as a vice, which flies in the face of living a Christian life of charity. When I learned that many libertarians at the seminar agreed with her views on morality, I began to question if libertarianism and Christianity could ever be compatible.

At the evening reception, I chatted with a peer who told me he did not think it was possible to be both a libertarian and a Christian. "Libertarianism is rational. Faith in God is not," he told me. Maybe I *was* at a pagan-inspired festival in the desert.

At the libertarian seminar, my Christian worldview was the minority in a sea of agnostics. I wondered if a Christian really *should* or even *could* be a libertarian. At the same time, I was growing more attracted to a libertarian political philosophy and believed many aspects were compatible with a Christian worldview—such as the emphasis on natural rights, the imperfect view of human nature, and the corrupting temptations of power. I wondered, is it possible, then, to reach the same endpoint of political liberty from two very different worldviews?

To figure this out, I needed to get to the bottom of two questions: (1) *Why are there so many non-Christian libertarians?* and (2) *Why aren't there more libertarian Christians?*

4. 1 Cor 6:19–20

WHY ARE THERE SO MANY NON-CHRISTIAN LIBERTARIANS?

Libertarians Might Assume Christianity Means Choosing Faith over Reason.

Growing up in a pocket of the evangelical community, I experienced an emphasis of faith over reason. Sometimes, it seemed as if the answer to nearly all of my questions was, "Because the Bible says so." Faith over reason. Belief over critical thinking. That was my experience as an inquisitive young adult. While this is certainly not the experience of all evangelicals, libertarian blogger Cathy Reisenwitz gave voice to this mentality when she said, "[The] attitude of being threatened by and discouraging questioning and critical thinking is, I think, one source of the great schism of libertarianism and Christianity."[5]

Faith and reason actually need each other. We cannot have one without the other. Blessed Pope John Paul II says in his encyclical *Fides et Ratio,* "Faith and reason are like two wings on which the human spirit rises to the contemplation of truth."

We all need reason to build a solid foundation for our faith. Yet faith requires taking a step beyond human reason, and many of the greatest intellectuals are uncomfortable doing so.

While many Christian traditions embrace reason, natural law, philosophy, and the sciences, I suspect many libertarians find it difficult to take that leap of faith from the reason in which they are so firmly grounded. When it comes to the subject of God for many intellectual libertarians, they may be tempted to believe the only logical conclusion is agnosticism. Although, opponents of Christianity often do not acknowledge they are also accepting facts, ideas, and concepts beyond what their own powers of reason and observation can validate.

Every belief system rests on faith. There are presuppositions behind everything we believe. Even the news article you read over a cup of coffee this morning required faith that the reporter was telling the truth. Theoretical knowledge, if accepted, requires faith. Laws of logic, scientific theories, mathematical abstractions, and philosophical concepts all require faith.

5. Reisenwitz, "Jesus is Still My Homeboy."

Libertarians Might Assume Christians Want to Force Their Morals on Others.

When you think of Christians in the public square, what's the first thought that comes to mind? Abortion clinic picketing? Anti-gay marriage signs waving in the air?

Many libertarians I've spoken with say they view Christians as a political cohort insistent on turning their morals into law for everyone, which they see as a threat to their own liberty and inherently inconsistent with libertarianism. For this reason, they recoil from the Christian right and run the other direction.

A friend once told me that as a libertarian, he could never be a Christian because he views the church as a top-down authority requiring submission to an absolute morality (I guess the concept of church reminded him of a totalitarian regime). I've met libertarian Christians who are anti-institutional across the board and opt for *home churches* for this very reason. Yet I would argue that even the most top-down church is compatible with a bottom-up, limited government within a libertarian political framework, since the church is a voluntary institution and the government is not.

As for whether or not Christianity means forcing morality on others through the law, I'll let Taylor Barkley explain that more in chapter 3.

WHY AREN'T THERE MORE LIBERTARIAN CHRISTIANS?

Some Christians Link Libertarianism to a Morally Bankrupt Worldview.

If you asked me what I thought a libertarian stood for before I knew what I know now, I probably would have responded with an answer involving drug use, gay marriage, radical individualism, and moral relativism. Cue the loud warning horn and flashing red lights.

Theologian and president of Southern Baptist Theological Seminary, Al Mohler, says as a conservative, he understands libertarianism as defined by exaltation of the ego, freedom from all moral restraints, and secular humanism. To the libertarian, liberty is the chief aim of life—it's a virtue, an end in and of itself.[6]

---

6. Roys, "Can a Christian Be Libertarian?"

Some libertarians do think that way, but as Taylor will outline in chapter 3, to assume libertarians are morally bankrupt ego worshippers misses the point of true libertarianism. In a liberty-centric political framework, freedom is only a means to an end. It's a prerequisite, a necessary foundation to society, that makes human flourishing possible.

Once we have freedom, then, what do we do with it? For the libertarian Christian, liberty is an opportunity to freely choose true Christian virtue. Worshiping and knowing God is still the chief aim of life, not radical individualism.

Christian economist Wilhelm Röpke argues that we need a morally sound culture to sustain liberty.[7] Along those lines, C.S. Lewis says that it is freedom that makes any goodness in this world worth having.[8] So, think of virtue and liberty like a moral sandwich: virtue presupposes liberty, and liberty in return sustains true virtue. Liberty and virtue need each other.

The Social Justice Movement Currently Dominates Christian Political Discourse.

Growing up in evangelical churches near military bases for the better half of my childhood, I assumed every church-going Christian was a registered Republican. I was a product of the evangelical right, and it was nearly impossible to understand how Christians could vote for a Democrat and still call themselves Christian.

The 2008 presidential election burst my conservative evangelical bubble. While some of my Christian friends in college were openly conservative, most did not like talking about politics, and the rest were voting for Barack Obama.

I realized something was changing in my generation of Christians, and it wasn't just that more were getting Bible verse tattoos, growing facial hair, and voting for progressive leaders. They were rebelling against the non-denominational megachurch politics of their childhood.

Author of *Hipster Christianity: When Church and Cool Collide*, Brett McCracken says Christian hipsters are rebelling against the church culture wars they were raised in, described as "the stereotypical evangelical church of the 80s–90s: the Republican, middle class, abortion-clinic-picketing, anti-gay, anti-welfare, legalistic, not-so-interested-in-art-or-books WASP

7. Röpke, *A Humane Economy*, 35.
8. Lewis, *Mere Christianity*, 47–48.

evangelical."[9] This rebellion fueled the rise of the evangelical social justice movement.

With the rise of Christian hipsterdom in the 2000s came the rise of the social justice movement, driven by evangelical thought leaders like Jim Wallis, Ron Sider, Lisa Sharon Harper, and Shane Claiborne. Rather than focusing on abortion or marriage issues as promoted by conservative evangelical groups like Focus on the Family, these leaders focus on poverty issues, human trafficking, the environment, and racial justice. They challenge capitalism, big business, and war.

Between 2009 and 2012, a Lifeway study showed increased church involvement in addressing poverty issues. Pastors said they gave more sermons on the topic of poverty and indicated an increase in congregational participation in service projects.[10]

The progress the social justice movement has made in addressing poverty is encouraging and much needed, though the prescriptive solution is one reminiscent of the theologically liberal Social Gospel movement in the early twentieth century. This Protestant movement was led by Walter Rauschenbusch, who was very critical of capitalism and promoted a form of Christian socialism as the means to achieve justice on earth.

Many evangelical social justice activists today echo Rauschenbusch. They associate capitalism with a greedy, selfish, superficial version of the American Dream. They believe our call to care for the poor requires government intervention—an expansion of public programs to truly answer our call to care for the most disadvantaged in society.

Forthcoming research from Institute for Faith, Work & Economics (IFWE) and the Barna Group found 56 percent of 18–30 year olds believe it's the government's job to care for the poor, as opposed to the church and private charities (28 percent) and the free market (16 percent).[11] Social justice leaders call for state intervention and often pursue policy goals that are fundamentally opposed to principles of liberty.

Jacqueline Isaacs, author of the first chapter, and I attended the 2015 Justice Conference in Chicago, one of the largest biblical and social justice conferences in the country. The conference drew together three thousand Christian leaders, justice practitioners, students, and learners from all over

---

9. McCracken, "The Economics of Hipsterdom."

10. Stetzer, "New Research."

11. "Christian Millennials Fighting Poverty." The Institute for Faith, Work & Economics (working paper).

the world to discuss issues surrounding faith and social justice. I'm not sure if I was or wasn't surprised to see Dr. Cornel West, a self-proclaimed Christian socialist, on the list of speakers at the evangelical conference.

Not a single Christian businessman was invited to speak about how many jobs they have provided for the poor through innovation and wealth creation. No headlining speaker dared mention the power of free enterprise and what it has done to lift whole nations out of poverty.

According to the World Bank, in 1981, 52 percent of the developing world's population lived in extreme poverty, as defined as living on less than $1.25 a day. By 2010, the percentage was cut by more than half (21 percent).[12] This positive shift is largely credited to open trade and free enterprise (Leah Hughey will continue this discussion in chapter 5).

But never mind that. Political principles of a just rule of law, individual rights, and economic freedom don't get the same play at evangelical student conferences. The social justice movement seems to dominate political discourse in Christian circles today, especially on college campuses, leaving political liberty off the mainstream radar.

It's important that Christians think critically about political principles, because these ideas have an incredible impact on the world. They have the power to either dodge or cause humanitarian crises. Political philosophy deals with whether or not people will continue struggling in poverty, crime, and disease perpetuated by harmful institutions or if they will be liberated toward a better, though imperfect, future. Economic freedom alone results in higher life expectancy, lower levels of infant mortality, better education, cleaner environments, better-protected civil liberties, higher incomes and employment, less child labor, and an overall higher quality of life. [13]

So then, is it possible to reach the same endpoint of political liberty from two very different worldviews? Understanding why so few libertarians seemed to identify as Christian was the beginning of my intellectual investigation, which ultimately pointed me to a confident yes. I believe you can be both a libertarian and a Christian for reasons the authors in this book will flesh out. As it turns out, I was not alone.

12. Beegle, et al., "The State of the Poor."
13. Bradley, "Five Reasons Christians."

LIBERTARIANISM IS ON THE RISE
IN THE CHRISTIAN COMMUNITY

Libertarianism is the most rapidly growing political affiliation in the early twenty-first century. The Gallup Governance Survey found 18 percent of Americans in the electorate identified as libertarian in 2004. In 2015, that number increased to 27 percent.[14] Libertarians are also young. According to a Public Religion Research Institute (PRRI), in 2013, the average age of a libertarian is 44 compared to the national average of 47.[15]

Students for Liberty was founded in 2008 to mobilize young libertarians. In 2016, it boasted over three thousand student groups across the globe in every inhabited continent. Popularized by Ron Paul's 2008 presidential campaign, the "liberty movement" is a reflection of growing distrust in political institutions and political leadership in Washington, especially in the millennial cohort.[16] Young people in the early twenty-first century crave autonomy, creativity, and innovation—exactly what the liberty movement fights for.

As the rise of the social justice movement indicates, young Christians are becoming more concerned about economic issues, not just social issues. They wrestle with questions like, "Is wealth creation virtuous or evil? What's the Christian view of income inequality? What's the best way to alleviate poverty?" Many are jaded with the culture wars they grew up with in the eighties and nineties and are, therefore, less likely to call themselves Republican or Democrat. Young Christians are searching for a third political avenue without compromising their Christian faith.

Though polls show millennials are less religious than previous generations, still 65 percent identify as Christian. Even though only one millennial in four actually attends church,[17] when it comes to importance of religion, prayer, belief in God, believing that the Bible is the word of God, and faith among those affiliated with a religious denomination, millennials look similar to previous generations when they were the same age.[18]

With an exploding population of young people considering themselves libertarian, over two-thirds of millennials calling themselves Christian, and

14. Boaz, "Gallup Finds More Libertarians in the Electorate."
15. Grossman, "Survey: Libertarian Numbers."
16. Cillizza, "Millennials Don't Trust Anyone."
17. Philips, "Millennials Are Spiritually Diverse."
18. "Religion Among the Millennials."

a generation passionate about entrepreneurship, innovation, fighting poverty, and economic justice, the cultural climate of American youth in the early twenty-first century is ripe for the unlikely intersection of Christianity and libertarianism.

Although many might assume that libertarians and Christians do not mix, libertarians are growing in number, even among Christian circles. The aforementioned PRRI study found that 42 percent of libertarians identify with a Christian denomination (27 percent mainline protestant, 23 percent evangelical, 11 percent Catholic, and 4 percent another Christian affiliation).[19]

In a 2012 *Relevant Magazine* article, Caryn Rivadeneira writes on the rise of the libertarian Christian in light of Ron Paul's upswing in popularity in the 2008 and 2012 GOP presidential primaries. "The surprising surge of support Ron Paul enjoys from young Americans—and young Christians—suggests that perhaps the libertarian-leaning aren't so far off in right field after all," Rivadeneira says.[20]

When Senator Ted Cruz dropped out of the 2016 GOP presidential primary race and left Donald Trump to later secure the Republican nomination, many conservative voters responded by burning their GOP registration cards on social media. Yet influential evangelical leaders, including Focus on the Family founder James Dobson, Liberty University president Jerry Falwell, and theologian Wayne Grudem, sang Trump's praises, leaving some Christian voters scratching their heads. It may not be a coincidence that the first Libertarian Party debate aired on Fox News the same year. The political climate is ripe for Christians, who voted Republican in the past, to begin searching for a new political home.

Today, Christians from the left and right are turning to libertarianism because they believe principles of limited government and individual freedom are compatible with biblical principles.

UNDERCOVER CHRISTIANS AT A LIBERTARIAN CONFERENCE

When I worked for IFWE, the organization sponsored the International Students for Liberty Conference (ISFLC) three years in a row. Though

19. Ibid.

20. Rivadeneira, "Rise of Christian Libertarians."

IFWE is not a libertarian organization, my colleagues and I were excited to engage in conversations about Christianity and economic freedom.

As the unlikely Christian exhibitors at the conference, I met more than one confused student who asked me, "Why are you here?" One student, Luke, thanked us for bringing a faith-based conversation to the conference with relief that he wasn't the only Christian in the room. Another, Theo, asked me how to explain to his Baptist parents why he no longer considers himself a Republican. Audrey asked me the best way to explain to her non-Christian libertarian friends why she doesn't agree with Ayn Rand's moral philosophy. Lauren outed herself as the only Christian at her libertarian organization. A few moments later, Annie, who worked at the same organization as Lauren, said *she* thought she was the only Christian in her office.

Did you catch that? These two young women thought they were the only Christians working at the same libertarian organization. I wish I could have introduced them to each other.

At conservative conferences like CPAC, exhibition halls seem to be filled with faith-based groups promoting Christian values. The same is not true for libertarian conferences. Maybe libertarian Christians assume they are alone, surrounded by intelligent agnostics ready to school them in an argument on the irrationality of a benevolent God. *Christians, you don't have to hide anymore.*

At ISFLC, IFWE organized panels on Christian topics, including *Why Christians Should Embrace Economic Freedom* and *Ayn Rand vs. Jesus*. Nearly each time, we attracted more students than chairs in the room. "Undercover" libertarian Christians are starved for conversation on the topics—an opportunity I believe the liberty movement was missing until Norman Horn organized the first Christians for Liberty Conference in 2014. The annual conference is an encouraging start to this much-needed conversation.

When I was offered the opportunity to present at the 2014 ISFLC in Washington, DC, I asked five like-minded peers to join me, and they are the authors you will meet in this book. The six of us sat on a panel titled *Jesus, Morality, and Liberty: Is Christian Morality Coercive?* The response from the students was overwhelmingly encouraging. This book is an attempt to extend that conversation across the country. With that in mind, there are three things you should know as you dive into this book.

First, the authors are all "libertarian Christians," but this is a term of convenience. It is not our intention to separate one "type" of Christian from the rest with an adjective, so we invite you to read this term as "a Christian who also happens to be a libertarian." Make no mistake: we are Christians first and libertarians second. We are libertarians *because* we are Christians.

Second, we believe we are called to freedom. When Paul told the Galatians they were "called to freedom,"[21] he was talking about freedom in Christ, freedom to follow him and become more like him. We cannot assume Paul meant anything more than this.

It is also important to remember that if Christ was who he said he was, it changes *everything*. He doesn't just change individual souls. He changes whole cultures and institutions, families and businesses, the arts and sciences, and economics and politics. Christ's redemptive work is one of total salvation that extends into every area of our lives. If it is true that humans suffer at the hands of totalitarian regimes and prosper in free societies, God cares about that. Christians, therefore, cannot ignore the role political systems play in our lives.

We believe God designed mankind to be free in more ways than one. There is no perfect form of government on this side of eternity, but we believe mankind flourishes more abundantly under a free society. Most importantly, we affirm that God cares about all these things: our wellbeing, our internal *and* external freedoms, and the governments we live under.

Finally, our intentions are not to explain why a Christian *should* be a libertarian but rather to show that reconciliation between these two seemingly unrelated worlds of libertarianism and Christianity is possible—not through our impressive academic credentials, but through our own personal accounts as young libertarian Christians wrestling with these very ideas ourselves.

From Catholic to Calvinist and representing thought across the libertarian spectrum, we bring to you the two most beloved dinner table topics in the most unlikely of ways. How can you be both a Christian and a libertarian? We begin with the story of creation and one young woman's journey.

21. Gal 5:13

BIBLIOGRAPHY

Ballor, Jordan. "Lord Acton on Catholic and Modern Views of Liberty." *The Acton Institute.* http://blog.acton.org/archives/57615-lord-acton-on-catholic-and-modern-views-of-liberty.html.

Beegle, Kathleen, Pedro Olinto, Carlos Sobrado, and Hiroki Uematsu. "The State of the Poor: Where Are the Poor and Where Are They Poorest?" *The World Bank.* http://siteresources.worldbank.org/EXTPREMNET/Resources/EP125.pdf.

Boaz, David. "Gallup Finds More Libertarians in the Electorate." *Cato Institute,* February 10, 2016. http://www.cato.org/blog/gallup-finds-more-libertarians-electorate.

———. "Libertarianism." *Encyclopædia Britannica Online,* accessed August 1, 2016. https://www.britannica.com/topic/libertarianism-politics.

Bradley, Anne Rathbone. "Five Reasons Christians Should Embrace Economic Freedom." *The Institute for Faith, Work & Economics,* July 31, 2013. https://tifwe.org/resource/five-reasons-christians-should-embrace-economic-freedom/.

Cillizza, Chris. "Millennials Don't Trust Anyone. That's a Big Deal." *The Washington Post,* April 30, 2015. https://www.washingtonpost.com/news/the-fix/wp/2015/04/30/millennials-dont-trust-anyone-what-else-is-new/.

Grossman, Cathy Lynn "Survey: Libertarian Numbers Are Small but Their Social, Political Clout Is Growing." *The Salt Lake Tribune,* October 29, 2013. http://archive.sltrib.com/story.php?ref=/sltrib/lifestyle/57056874–80/percent-libertarians-party-tea.html.csp.

Lewis, C.S. Mere Christianity. New York: HarperCollins, 2001.

McCracken, Brett. "The Economics of Hipsterdom: An Interview with Brett McCracken." *Remnant Culture,* November 16, 2010. http://remnantculture.com/2144-the-economics-of-hipsterdom-an-interview-with-brett-mccracken.

Philips, Rob. "Millennials Are Spiritually Diverse." *LifeWay,* April 27, 2010. http://www.lifeway.com/Article/LifeWay-Research-finds-American-millennials-are-spiritually-diverse.

Reisenwitz, Cathy. "Jesus is Still My Homeboy. But Like All of My Relationships, Ours Is a Weird One." *Sex and the State,* July 15, 2013. http://cathyreisenwitz.com/jesus-is-still-my-homeboy-but-like-all-of-my-relationships-ours-is-a-weird-one/.

"Religion Among the Millennials." *Pew Research Center,* February 17, 2010. http://www.pewforum.org/2010/02/17/religion-among-the-millennials/.

Rivadeneira, Caryn. "Rise of Christian Libertarians." *Relevant Magazine,* January 27, 2012. http://www.relevantmagazine.com/life/current-events/op-ed-blog/28097-the-rise-of-christian-libertarianism#3jckc7upI4BoMDzL.99.

Röpke, Wilhelm. *A Humane Economy: The Social Framework of the Free Market.* Wilmington, Delaware: Intercollegiate Studies Institute, 1998.

Roys, Julie, Al Mohler, and Norman Horn. "Can a Christian Be Libertarian?" *Up for Debate.* Moody Radio. March 5, 2016, radio broadcast, 46:50. http://www.moodyradio.org/Up-for-Debate/2016/2016–03-05-Can-a-Christian-be-Libertarian/.

Stetzer, Ed. "New Research: Protestants Increase Involvement in Social Justice." *Christianity Today,* October 9, 2013. http://www.christianitytoday.com/edstetzer/2013/october/new-research-protestants-increase-involvement-in-social-jus.html

1

Can I Be a Libertarian Christian?
Jacqueline Isaacs

Fundamentally, Christianity is about our freedom, or rather our ability to choose to have a relationship with God, our choice to believe in Him. Given the importance of that underlying principle, I have chosen to live my life in that manner as well. To my understanding, freedom in our everyday, utterly practical lives means the free exchange of goods and ideas, the freedom to speak one's mind, the freedom to travel, the freedom to pursue happiness, the freedom to reap what one sows, and the freedom to come to one's own terms with God.

So going back to our initial question—does that make me a Christian libertarian?

I think it just makes me a Christian.

—JACQUELINE ISAACS[1]

T hose words were written by me in the midst of a personal journey, one I'm very much still on, to find peace between my Christian faith and my libertarian political philosophy. It started when I booked a one-way flight from my hometown of Tulsa, Oklahoma, to Washington, DC.

1. Isaacs, "A Christian Libertarian Part 2."

It was January 2011, and I had just graduated in December. I had known since my earlier semester studying and interning in Washington that it was where I wanted to launch my career.

As a political science major, there weren't many job opportunities in the Midwest, but my internship at the American Enterprise Institute (AEI) introduced me to the world of public policy, and I was determined to work at a think tank researching and promoting the ideas of freedom. When the wheels of my one-way flight touched down at Reagan National Airport, that dream life seemed like it was almost reality.

When the sun rose in the nation's capital the next morning, I faced reality. I didn't have a job lined up, and life in Washington was proving to be a mixed bag of emotions. I was newly single, the job I thought I would land fell through, and I was quickly realizing that Washington was an expensive place to live.

In a desperate move, I googled "think tanks in DC" and found an alphabetized list on *Wikipedia*. I started with the *a*'s and sent my resume to every think tank that I thought I could possibly agree with enough to work for, whether they had a job opening or not.

When I reached the *c*'s, the Competitive Enterprise Institute offered me an internship with a stipend. While the stipend worked out to significantly less than minimum wage, in the moment, it was close enough to my dream job to thrill me. I was off to make the world safe for freedom.

At some point, that internship turned into a full-time job at that same think tank. I was researching policy, but I also paid my dues by answering the phones, sorting mail, and making coffee. I worked with a wide range of personalities, and it quickly became apparent that I may have been the only Christian in the office. There might have been others, but if there were, they didn't talk about their faith like I did. After all, I had just arrived from the Bible Belt.

My coworkers and I had many conversations about faith, and besides feeling a bit like a novelty, I felt well-accepted. I was quite surprised then when one of my self-described agnostic coworkers attempted to explain to me that one couldn't be both religious and libertarian. This was probably the first time I had heard an opinion that faith and libertarianism were not compatible. In the moment, I was quite concerned. Did this mean my coworkers didn't accept me? Did I not meet some libertarian purity test?

I noticed most of the people who worked at libertarian think tanks in Washington did seem to be non-religious. This was odd to me. When I was involved in local politics in Oklahoma and Texas, being pro-small government seemed inherent to being a Christian.

While I expected living in Washington to challenge my worldview, I didn't expect the intersection of my faith and my libertarian political philosophy to be the skirmish point.

After that conversation with my coworker, I took a moment to write down what he said. So while the following is not a direct quote from him about why faith and libertarianism are irreconcilable, I believe it correctly captures his argument:

> Free individuals will tend to pursue their rational self-interest. This is a core tenet of libertarianism. If voluntary society is to outperform statism, reason and logic must be rewarded and valued. By instructing people to believe in ideas without any empirical or logical basis, religion detracts from rational behavior in ways that are destructive to freedom.

This left me with many questions—about my faith, about my libertarianism, and about my career. I began working through these ideas in my new column with the American Enterprise Institute's Project on Values and Capitalism.

Reflecting on my personal experience, as I grew in my understanding of the Christian faith, I became increasingly libertarian. So I assumed that I would find a lot of support for my idea of cohesion between my faith and my philosophy. I was sure that my coworker was just an outlier.

That was when I wrote about believing in individual freedom, saying, "Does that make me a Christian libertarian? I think it just makes me a Christian."

However, as I was working through these ideas, I received a response from another Christian writer at the Acton Institute who responded with his take on "Christian libertarians." He argued that there were the following five types of Christian libertarians:

Type 5. Those who are not-all-that Christian or not-all-that libertarian

Type 4. Christians who are really conservatives, but don't like the label "conservative"

Type 3. Those for whom the "Christian" in Christian libertarian is a weak modifier

Type 2. Those who mash the two words together and think that "since they are able to hold both views without their heads exploding, they assume the two views must be compatible."

Type 1. Those who have developed a consistent philosophy in which libertarianism and Christianity are fully compatible. He quickly noted, however "although I'm not sure I've ever met a Type 1—and I'm not sure it's even possible."[2]

It was undeniable. I, like everyone who considers himself or herself a libertarian Christian, was finding myself challenged by both associations.

I needed to do some deep thinking about how my faith interacted with my political philosophy. I needed to answer the question, "Can I be a Christian and a libertarian?" Because the world around me was arguing intensely that I could not.

A GOSPEL UNDERSTANDING OF HUMAN NATURE

My journey through theology and philosophy to answer that question has been long, sometimes messy, but ultimately uplifting and has strengthened both my faith and my libertarianism—and it certainly is not over.

From where I'm currently at on my journey, there are a few things of which I am completely convinced. First, our human nature is defined by the four-chapter gospel of creation, fall, redemption, and consummation. Second, through this lens, we can see that we are made to emulate God's creativity, to live in relationship and community, and to receive salvation through grace that is individual and voluntary. Third, this gospel understanding of human nature should be the foundation of our political philosophy.

So what is the four-chapter gospel? I certainly hadn't heard of it until I began this journey. As it turns out, it's an idea as old as the New Testament.

Theologian John Stott introduces and explains this concept saying that he "personally found it yet more helpful to adopt the framework provided by scripture as a whole."[3] Adopting this framework is not only helpful for Christians, but also essential because it protects against the fallacy of *proof-texting* which Stott defines as "the notion that we can settle every doctrinal and ethical issue by quoting a single, isolated text, whereas God has given

2. Carter, "What is a Christian Libertarian?"

3. Stott, *Issues Facing Christians Today*, 62

us a comprehensive revelation."[4] My coauthor Jason Hughey addresses the problem of proof-texting in more detail in chapter 2, but I agree with Stott that the Christian mind must reject this selective view of scripture and instead saturate itself in the "fullness of scripture."[5]

The result of this fullness of scripture, is an understanding of "the fourfold scheme of biblical history."[6] Stott explains that, "the Bible divides human history into epochs, which are marked not by the rise and fall of empires, dynasties or civilizations, but by four major events: the creation, the fall, the redemption, and the consummation."[7]

Hugh Whelchel, author and executive director of the Institute for Faith, Work & Economics, references New Testament scholar N.T. Wright in describing the same fullness of scripture as a story or a narrative that God Almighty is telling throughout history. I've found the following by Whelchel to be a helpful way to remember the four major acts of the story (though he uses the term "restoration" for the final chapter instead of "consummation"):

> Creation: The way things were.
> Fall: The way things are.
> Redemption: The way things could be.
> Restoration: The way things will be.[8]

"In the beginning, God created the heavens and the earth."[9] The very opening scene of scripture tells us about the world that God created—the way things were. That first book of the Bible goes on to tell us about the fall—the way things are now. We see that things are no longer perfect; everything in the world, including ourselves, is broken.

In the aftermath of that brokenness, God still loved the world so much that he gave his only son, that whoever believes in him should not perish but have everlasting life instead.[10] In the Gospels, as well as throughout the New Testament, we learn about God's answer to the fall. Through his redemption, we get a glimpse of the way things could be again. Ultimately, throughout Paul's Epistles and John's book of Revelation, we learn about

4. Ibid., 62
5. Ibid., 62
6. Ibid., 62
7. Ibid., 62
8. Whelchel, "Our Mission."
9. Gen 1:1
10. John 3:16

the consummation (or restoration), the vision for how the world will be restored again after Christ's return.

Through all the books and authors of the Bible, we are given an explanation for the human condition that starts with the creation of the cosmos, ends with its renewal, and in between those bookends "offers an interpretation of the meaning of all history."[11] Nothing in our lives escapes the scope of this story. Nothing is left unaccountable to the storyteller.

While it may seem like an odd place to begin a book about libertarian Christians, I believe it is the only place to begin. All of our political thinking is held in this story, somewhere in between Christ's redemption and the world's restoration, predicated by our creation and our fall. We are called to live in this story boldly. Take courage, for through this four-chapter story, Jesus tells us how he has overcome the world.[12] Can we live like he has in *every* area of our lives—including our thinking about politics?

Understanding the four-chapter gospel can radically transform how we live our lives, engage in the public square, and consider political philosophy. It tells a unique story about human nature that should excite and challenge us.

Scottish theologian Stephen Neill was a man who was excited and challenged by this Christian story. He spent many years as a missionary to India before returning to Britain where he made major contributions to train missionaries to go to various people groups around the world. A significant theme of his work is what Neill defines as the uniqueness of Christianity. "More perhaps than any other form of religion or philosophy," Neill explains, "the Christian faith takes the human situation seriously. It never doubts for a moment that it is a great and glorious thing to be a human being . . . Jesus came to show what human life really is."[13]

When God shone a light on what it meant to be human, he didn't berate us for our brokenness; he brought hope for the hopeless. Jesus came to show us how to flourish. Andy Crouch, author and executive producer of *Christianity Today*, points out that this is the epitome of human flourishing. "No human being ever embodied flourishing more than Jesus of Nazareth," says Crouch.[14]

---

11. Whelchel, "Our Mission."

12. John 16:33

13. Neill, *The Christian Faith*, 22–23.

14. Crouch, *Strong and Weak*, 16.

Neill agrees that this is the significance of the gospel, the highlight of the human life, but Neill uses a different word. Instead of *flourishing*, he calls it *freedom*. He says, "The characteristic dimension of human existence is freedom. On this narrow sand-bank between existence and nonexistence, between coercion and chaos, God has withdrawn his hand so far as to make a space in which we can be really, though not unconditionally, free. In Jesus we see what a free man looks like."[15]

This is the significance of the four-chapter gospel. Before we can attempt to derive from scripture what we as Christians ought to be doing in the world, we need a solid foundational understanding of who scripture says *we* are. In my journey, I wanted to understand more about this profound story that has led many theologians to the conclusion that the fullness and flourishing of humanity is freedom.

Let's start with the first of the four chapters, creation, and let's also set aside questions about how literally the creation story of Genesis is intended to be taken. Some very important facets of human nature that come out of the biblical telling of creation are indisputable to Christians.

In the beginning, humanity, male and female, were made immortal in the image of God.[16] The *Imago Dei*. We are made to create as God created. We are given dominion over nature to infuse it with our God-given creativity. After the land was separated from the water, the birds were put in the air and the fish in sea. Even after animals were made to roam the face of the earth, God breathed life into humanity. We were made to be in relationship with each other, in command of nature, and in love with our Creator. God said that his handiwork in us was "very good."[17]

Humanity was created with authority, what Crouch calls "capacity for meaningful action." [18] This authority is uniquely given to humanity, male and female, by God as his image bearers in this world. This "godlikeness of humankind" deeply and profoundly describes humanity. From the creation story, Stott pulls out several important characteristics. Men and women are . . .

1. Rational and moral beings (able to understand and respond to God's commands)

2. Responsible beings (exercising dominion over nature)

15. Neill, *The Christian Faith*, 22–23.

16. Gen 1:27

17. Gen 1:31

18. Crouch, *Strong and Weak*, 39.

3. Social beings (with capacity to love and be loved)

4. Spiritual beings (finding their highest fulfilment in knowing and worshipping their Creator)[19]

C.S. Lewis famously described our godlikeness in *The Weight of Glory*, saying "There are no ordinary people. You have never talked to a mere mortal. Nations, cultures, arts, civilizations—these are mortal, and their life is to ours as the life of a gnat."[20]

Do not miss how powerful this is. Understanding what creation says about humanity and the value of our creative work, places an importance on a whole host of topics in our political philosophy. We ought to value systems in society that protect and reward our work. We ought to strive to let the creators create—create art, create jobs, create technological advances, and more. Using our God-given gifts and talents reflects God as the ultimate Creator and brings him glory. What I'm touching on here about humanity engaging our Imago Dei to increase flourishing and bring glory to God, my coauthor, Leah Hughey will flesh out in chapter 4, and it is deeply rooted in the chapter of creation in Genesis.

Of course, all is not as perfect as it was when God first created the world. The story of the four-chapter gospel goes on to tell us how humanity first sinned and became separated from God. The first humans "listened to Satan's lies, instead of God's truth,"[21] creating a schism over which we can never go back.

Not only are we suffering from our alienation from our Creator, but all of our important relationships have been shattered. In their ground-breaking book on addressing poverty, *When Helping Hurts*, Christian economists Steve Corbett and Brian Fikkert claim that the fall broke four key relations: our relationship with God, our relationship with ourselves, our relationship with others, and our relationship with the rest of creation. These relationships are grounded in creation, and they inform all of the aspects of our lives. When they were whole, humanity flourished. Now that they are broken, we cannot experience the "fullness of life that God intended."[22]

We were made in in the image of God, with all of the glorious benefits thereof, and we gave it up. We were made for perfect freedom, but sin

19. Stott, *Issues Facing Christians Today*, 62.

20. Lewis, *The Weight of Glory*, 46.

21. Stott, *Issues Facing Christians Today*, 62.

22. Corbett, *When Helping Hurts*, 54–55.

ruined the perfection of God's creation. This is the greatest tragedy mankind has endured, and it has scarred what it means to be human. We were made by God, to bear his image and to enjoy him forever, but now we live apart from him. Our desire to worship God is now turned to worshiping ourselves. Our desire for creation is now turned to destruction. Our desire for holiness is now turned to evil. The endless fight against meaninglessness that has marked our history stems from this.

The fall really happened, and it has powerful implications for how humans live together. We ought to be hesitant to entrust too much power to *any* person or group of people to rule over others as these people are ingrained with evil. James Madison famously described the paradox that the fall created for government saying in Federalist 51, "If men were angels, no government would be necessary. If angels were to govern men . . . controls on government would not be necessary."[23]

While we still bear God's image, the lasting impact of the fall is that we now do so imperfectly. Very imperfectly. God's image is just visible enough for us to sense that we were made for something more.

But this, thankfully, is only half of the story. God does not abandon us when the story reaches this conflict, when humanity seems lost. Because of the fall, we know that every one of us is sinful. We know that each of us have fallen short of the glory of God. We are in need of salvation, and we are utterly unable to save ourselves.

This can be hard for us to accept, because there are moments when we do feel in control of our lives. We like to make our own choices, blaze our own paths, and provide for ourselves. The truth is that we can labor our entire lives, and the labor will be in vain. Sowing the wind, and reaping the whirlwind.[24] We are part of the problem and cannot be the solution. The message of the gospel, the good news, is that salvation from our sins is offered through Christ Jesus.

Jesus Christ, God himself, became human flesh and lived among us.[25] Whereas we all live lives of broken relationships because of the fall, Jesus lived a life fully rooted in what humanity was created to be. We were destined to reap death and separation from God in hell for eternity for sowing brokenness all our lives, but Jesus sowed what we could not. He had perfect relationships with nature, with others, with himself, and with the Father.

23. Madison, *The Federalist Papers*, 319.
24. Hos 8:7
25. John 1:14

Having lived this life free of brokenness, Jesus made a way for us to be free by intervening in our demise. He traded his freedom for our death. This is the core message of Christianity—what we want everyone to know! We believe that, when we die, we will stand individually before God. We have hope in the fact that if we have put our trust in his salvation, Christ alone will be standing with us. Here we see in this central message of Christianity, the ideals of individual choice and voluntary action.

It is individual and voluntary not because of our effort, but because of Christ alone. He was the only person who had the authority to lay down his life and take it up again.[26] And he chose to do so. The person in whom we see what it truly means to be free made a choice and voluntarily suffered beyond all imagining, because he wanted the rest of us to experience what it means to be free too.

This is the third chapter—redemption. From the moment the fall happened, God had a plan, and he promised that the woman's seed would crush the serpent's head.[27] "Then in the fullness of time the Messiah came. With him the new age dawned, the kingdom of God broke in, the end began." Stott says, "Now today, through the death, resurrection and Spirit-gift of Jesus, God is fulfilling his promise of redemption and is remaking marred humankind, saving individuals and incorporating them into his new, reconciled community."[28]

Interestingly, redemption is not the end of the story either. There is one more chapter—what Stott calls the "consummation" and Whelchel calls "restoration." This is the final act of the story of scripture, which we are still looking forward to. At a time that only God the Father knows,[29] when the good news of the kingdom has been proclaimed throughout the whole world,[30] Jesus Christ will appear again. "He will raise the dead, judge the world, regenerate the universe and bring God's kingdom to its perfection. From it all pain, decay, sin, sorrow and death will be banished, and in it God will be glorified for ever."[31]

This gives us great hope. It tells us that God not only has a plan to redeem us from our sins, but he has a plan to restore us and the whole of

---

26. John 10:18
27. Gen 3:16
28. Stott, *Issues Facing Christians Today*, 63.
29. Matt 24:36
30. Matt 24:14
31. Stott, *Issues Facing Christians Today*, 63.

creation. "Meanwhile, we are living in between times," Stott warns, "between kingdom come and kingdom coming, between the 'now' and the 'then' of redemption, between the 'already' and the 'not yet.'"[32]

There is so much depth to this four-chapter gospel. What has been important to me as I stare into these deep waters is that Christianity starts with the individual, celebrates the individual's inherent dignity and opportunity for salvation, and grows outwardly into community and kingdom.

We, as Christians, should aim to live our lives in a manner that tells the truth about scripture. We should live out this glorious story as best we can. If we are living out this story in its fullness, we get closer to experiencing the fullness of humanity as God intended, and we can even begin to see glimpses of human flourishing. For example, God created everything out of nothing, and we can create economic value out of scarcity. God redeems us from our sins, and we work toward redeeming others from poverty, ignorance, and disease. God respects our freedom, even our freedom to disobey him, and we respect the freedom of others in our society.

This story also introduces us to the idea that Christianity is about voluntary action, because it is through this voluntary social engagement by which we develop individual virtue and emulate our Creator. It is through voluntary action that we bring flourishing to others.

The social obligations put forward in the New Testament are described as voluntary, yet we are extolled by the apostle Paul to use our freedom, our flourishing, to serve others. The apostle Paul said repeatedly, "though I am free from all, I have made myself a servant to all,"[33] and, "you were called to freedom . . . only do not use your freedom as an opportunity for the flesh, but through love serve one another"[34]

When you understand human nature as told by the four-chapter gospel, where humans bear the image of God and yet are fallen and that redemption is available to us but we are not yet fully restored, you can better value principles such as individual choice and voluntary action. With these principles, you begin to develop a worldview that recognizes the communal nature of flourishing taking shape in multiple spheres of authority—God, the individual, the church, the community, the family, and so on.

Jordan Ballor, of the Acton Institute, explains in his book *Get Your Hands Dirty* that each of these spheres of authority have various rights and

32. Ibid., 63.

33. 1 Cor 9:19

34. Gal 5:13

responsibilities and that balancing all of them appropriately is key to having "a rightly ordered life." It is a necessary condition, he argues, for flourishing both for individuals and for the communities in which they live.

Ballor describes an ordinate life as one that is "rightly ordered relative to other loves, regards, and interests."[35] With this framework, if a sphere of authority acts beyond its limits or does something that is the responsibility of another sphere, it is tyrannizing the sphere that is responsible for those actions. We see this most prominently when the government does things the church, the community, or individuals ought to be doing.

When we think about what the proper place of government is in society, we should seek "to properly relate the political to everything else (culture, business, family, charity, church)."[36] This conception of order speaks to what Wilhem Röpke describes in *A Humane Economy*, as "an order which fosters individual independence and responsibility as much as the public spirit which connects the individual with the community and limits his greed."[37]

Ballor also pulls from Lord Acton, a British historian and politician, who argued that liberty and good government were not mutually exclusive and in reality should be found together, because "liberty is not a means to a higher political end. It is itself the highest political end."[38]

"Notice the modifier 'political' in that quotation," Ballor says. "It makes all the difference in the world."[39] Certainly the other side of this coin is that the role for the individual should also be in its proper place. The liberty for which he argues is not the "libertine" ideal, so often conflated with the positions of those who favor limited government. My coauthor, Taylor Barkley, will go into more depth about libertarian versus libertine thinking in chapter 3.

This worldview, based on the four-chapter gospel of human nature, is what some might refer to as a conservative worldview, because as we discussed, the individual has rights and responsibilities. The church has rights and responsibilities. These responsibilities are what cause some libertarians

35. Ballor, *Get Your Hands Dirty*, 62.

36. Ibid., 206.

37. Röpke, *A Humane Economy*, 125.

38. Lord John Emerich Edward Dalberg Acton, "The History of Freedom in Antiquity" (1877), quoted in Jordan Ballor, *Get Your Hands Dirty*, 202.

39. Ibid., 202.

to reject faith, like my former coworker who first told me that my faith was incompatible with freedom.

If we hold this Christian worldview, which recognizes individuals as image bearers of God who are capable of significant authority and also recognize a more limited authority for government, it is completely compatible with libertarianism as understood as a political philosophy of limited government and free markets. In a similar manner, libertarianism as a political philosophy fits into other worldviews, such as the worldview of Objectivism, because a political philosophy is a subset of a worldview and not the totality of one.

The key is to understand that in our lives and in this book, my coauthors and I are Christians first. We have all become libertarians because of our Christian faith. Jason will offer a more complete definition of libertarianism in chapter 2, and I think it will be clear how the more robust definition of the political philosophy is not only compatible with a Christian worldview but is strengthened by scripture.

My journey to better understand my faith and my libertarianism has brought me back to the beginning where I hold both together. Now I confidently understand that instead of a Christian view of human nature fitting into a libertarian political philosophy, it is the libertarian political philosophy that fits into the Christian worldview as told by the four-chapter gospel.

Ultimately, being a libertarian Christian is acknowledging that the brokenness of our world includes ourselves, our political and social systems, and our intellectual constructs that we depend upon to make sense of this world. It is about being a Christian first and using scripture to inform our political thinking.

Now when I consider the question, "Can I be a Christian and a libertarian?" I reflect again on what I know to be true. First, human nature is defined by the four-chapter gospel of creation, fall, redemption, and consummation. Second, through this lens, we can see that we are made to emulate God's creativity, to live in relationship and community, and to receive salvation through grace that is individual and voluntary. Third, this gospel understanding of human nature should be the foundation of our political philosophy.

SO IS THERE AN ANSWER TO THE QUESTION?

At this point, now several years into my journey, I am adjusting my goals. While I have found that a Christian understanding of human nature, as told by the four-chapter gospel, supports several elements of libertarian philosophy, it does not holistically endorse any political philosophy. Friends of mine pressure me to choose a side because the values and faith that I so deeply believe in are in tension with the freedom I espouse. While this may be an oversimplification, when traditional Christian values and individual liberty come into tension (which they regularly do), political conservatives will default to protecting values, and libertarians will default to protecting liberty.

Instead of trying to make peace between my Christian faith and my libertarian political philosophy, I have shifted to trying to make peace with the inherent tension. As we have seen, many of the scholars cited so far have identified a tension. Stott talks about how we are "living in between times, between kingdom come and kingdom coming, between the 'now' and the 'then' of redemption, between the 'already' and the 'not yet.'"[40]

Crouch identifies the tension between our capacity for meaningful action and our exposure to meaningful risk, saying, "we image bearers are bone and flesh—strength and weakness, authority and vulnerability, together."[41] Corbett and Fikkert show how all of our relationships with God, others, ourselves, and the rest of creation, were made good but now are in tension. Ballor identifies the tension of holding authority for individuals and other social structures in right order.

This seems like a natural place to be as a Christian; after all, Christians are well acquainted with tension. Almost everything about the gospel is in tension. Our flesh is sinful, yet we are being sanctified. Christ's kingdom exists now, through the church, but is not yet in its fullness. Christ was 100 percent God and 100 percent man at the same time.

However, through the four-chapter gospel, we have an explanation for the tension. We were created in the Image of God, but we are fallen. We can be redeemed by accepting salvation through Christ, but we are still working toward being fully restored.

We know that we were made to live in communion with God where morality and liberty were in harmony. And we know that now, in our fallen,

---

40. Stott, *Issues Facing Christians Today*, 63.
41. Crouch, *Strong and Weak*, 45.

sinful, broken world full of fallen, sinful, broken people that just isn't possible. Yet.

When we examine our political philosophy and our faith and find tension, we ought not to be surprised. In fact, political scientist Don Devine claims that Christianity is to blame. "Christianity, however, rests on the claimed reality of a single event, the Incarnation, the assertion that God entered human existence to change it," argues Devine. "Whatever the explanation, freedom entered history in a dramatic way following this event, causing an enduring tension between liberty and order, state and church, love and power, and all the rest."[42]

Yet we also have an answer for the tension—the fourth chapter of restoration. As Christians, we believe that our story ends with Jesus Christ returning and restoring heaven and earth, reuniting our virtue and our freedom. As we wait, we can, through our faith and our faithful presence, hold the two in tension.

As you continue reading, my coauthors delve more deeply into the philosophical and theological underpinnings of being libertarian Christians. I hope that this four-chapter gospel understanding of human nature provides you with a solid framework in which to continue reading.

As for myself and from what I've learned in my journey, I firmly believe that we can embrace the tension and begin to synthesize the two in small ways that bring increasing flourishing to our society and glory to God.

42. Devine, *American's Way Back*, 155.

BIBLIOGRAPHY

Ballor, Jordan J. *Get Your Hands Dirty: Essays on Christian Social Thought (and Action)*. Eugene, OR: Wipf & Stock, 2013.

Carter, Joe. "What is a Christian Libertarian?" *Acton Institute Power Blog* (blog).

Corbett, Steve, and Fikkert, Brian. *When Helping Hurts: Alleviating Poverty without Hurting the Poor . . . and Yourself*. Chicago: Moody, 2012

Crouch, Andy. *Strong and Weak: Embracing a Life of Love, Risk & True Flourishing*. Downer's Grove, IL: InterVarsity, 2016.

Devine, Donald J. *American's Way Back: Reclaiming Freedom, Tradition, and Constitution*. Wilmington, Delaware: Intercollegiate Studies Institute, 2013.

Isaacs, Jacqueline. "A Christian Libertarian Part 2." *Values and Capitalism,* 2011. http://www.valuesandcapitalism.com/a-christian-libertarian-part-2/.

Lewis, C.S. *The Weight of Glory and Other Addresses*. New York, NY: HarperOne, 2001.

Madison, James, A. Hamilton, and J. Jay. *The Federalist Papers*. New York, NY: Signet Classic, 2003.

Neill, Stephen. *Christian Faith and Other Faiths: The Christian Dialogue with Other Religions*. 2nd ed. Downers Grove, IL: InterVarsity, 1984.

Röpke, Wilhelm. *A Humane Economy: The Social Framework of the Free Market*. Wilmington, DE: Intercollegiate Studies Institute, 1998.

Stott, John, R. McCloughry, and J. Wyatt. *Issues Facing Christians Today*. 4th ed. Grand Rapids, MI: Zondervan, 2006.

Whelchel, H. "Our Mission Is More than Sin Management: The Four Chapter Gospel and God's Grand Story of Redemption." *Institute for Faith, Work & Economics,* April 20, 2015. https://tifwe.org/our-mission-is-more-than-sin-management/.

2

What Does the Bible Say about Government?

Jason Hughey

Again I saw all the oppressions that are done under the sun. And behold, the tears of the oppressed, and they had no one to comfort them! On the side of their oppressors there was power, and there was no one to comfort them.

—THE BOOK OF ECCLESIASTES[1]

This lust of sovereignty disturbs and consumes the human race with frightful ills. By this lust Rome was overcome when she triumphed over Alba, and praising her own crime, called it glory. [. . .] Away, then, with these deceitful masks, these deluding whitewashes, that things may be truthfully seen and scrutinized."

—ST. AUGUSTINE, CITY OF GOD[2]

In November of 2000, I lived next to my radio. I tuned into the local news station 107.7 FM WTOP to listen for updates about the Florida presidential

---

1. Eccles 4:1
2. Augustine, *The City of God*, 86.

election recount and those very controversial "hanging chads." At the time, I was a homeschooled student, so I didn't have to worry about missing a class session or being late to PE. Like a die-hard football fan who has to watch every play of every game, I had to know what was happening on an hour-by-hour basis. The radio was always on, whether I pondered math homework, washed the dishes after dinner, or played a game of Risk with my brother. Since the future of the United States hung in the balance, I had no choice but to listen. At least, that's what my ten-year-old brain told me.

It might be hard to believe that, as a ten-year-old, the 2000 election between George W. Bush and Al Gore kept me at such rapt attention. Yet, it did, and I cared deeply about my opinions. I believed that, if Gore was elected, he would raise taxes, sign the Kyoto protocol, slow economic growth to a halt, strengthen abortion rights, and weaken the military. I knew that he was the vice president to Bill Clinton, who was not a good president and who lied about things that he did with a woman named Monica Lewinsky. In my mind, there was no way Al Gore could have been a good president for the United States.

In contrast, George W. Bush was a knight in shining cowboy boots. His rugged Texan charm, combined with his advocacy of small government, lower taxes, and the pro-life position, made an impact on me. I knew lower taxes would allow adults, like my parents, to keep more of their money, which would allow them to save for college, to invest in the stock market, and to buy a house. I knew the unborn were fully human and worthy of protection from violence—and I knew George W. Bush did as well. Ultimately, I believed that Bush was a thoroughly good man who cared deeply about the future of America, and his beliefs would help him govern as a wise and good president.

So I listened to the radio, waiting anxiously to hear about Florida's results. As the story unfolded, I identified the heroes and the villains, those who stood for Bush and those who stood for Gore. If someone asked me who the nine justices on the Supreme Court were, I rattled their names off immediately, like a baseball fan rattling off the starting lineup for his favorite team. I waited. I prayed. I listened. I waited some more.

You can imagine my elation when the Supreme Court delivered its decision in early December, essentially ensuring a Bush win in Florida and, consequently, a Bush presidency. I could not stop feeling grateful for Sandra Day O'Connor, Clarence Thomas, William Rehnquist, Antonin Scalia, and Anthony Kennedy. In my ten-year-old mind, those five justices helped the

United States dodge a major bullet, saving us from the disastrous potential reign of Al Gore.

It didn't take long for my childlike faith in President Bush to be rewarded. I firmly believed that his strong and swift response to 9/11 was essential to the maintenance of justice. Like the rest of the country, I was rocked to the core as I watched the smoke billow out of the World Trade Center and, shortly afterward, collapse to the ground in a cloud of debris. I was stirred by Bush's leadership and the symbols of firefighters and policemen rushing into the buildings to save every last person they could. So when it came down to it, I was all-in on the War on Terror. If I had been old enough, I would have joined the military immediately, no questions asked. I even remember talking with a couple of my friends about how we could join up and go fight the terrorists when we were old enough.

Despite my ardent support for President Bush, Republican policy agendas, and the war on terrorism, I distinctly remember a time when a possible chink in my neoconservative armor emerged. I was riding home with my mom from a piano practice session—and, of course, we were listening to 107.7 FM WTOP. The anchors were covering the Bush era wiretapping policies and some commentators were expressing concern that such policies violated privacy rights. I distinctly remember commenting to my mom, "That makes sense. I understand why President Bush is using wiretapping to keep us safe; however, if a president who was not as good as President Bush used such power, they could easily abuse it and use it to harm innocent people who they don't like." Of course, I naively still concluded that I was all right with the current policy because it was President Bush approving domestic surveillance.

My questions and personal musings continued to develop over the course of my high school years. From the ages of 13–18, I sunk myself into high school speech and debate competitions. High school debate became my competitive outlet—I wanted to not only be a good debater but one of the best debaters in my league. During this time, I debated issues of federal policy and ethical values, ranging from how to handle medical malpractice policy to whether or not democracy was an overvalued ideal of the US government.

In considering these topics, I had to force myself to structure arguments and defend given propositions by marshaling evidence and applying critical thinking. I learned that one could not simply assert that something was true, but one had to prove it. I learned that arguments, if they were to remain valid, couldn't contradict themselves. And I learned how to identify standards of value by which to assess trade-offs in a complex and messy world, which I increasingly came to understand was filled less with heroes and villains and more with confusing and complex people. As my preconceived narratives became less satisfying in the face of my growing appreciation of reality's complexity, I remained committed to understanding what was true, as any debater should. However, I realized that the truth was not always what it immediately appeared to be—and that developing a better perspective of the world required a commitment to evaluating one's presuppositions and comparing competing claims against empirical evidence and the laws of logic.

Somewhere along the line, the crack in my neoconservative armor expanded, as I trained myself to critically evaluate my beliefs through the mechanisms I learned in competitive debate. At the very end of high school, I attended a seminar run by the Foundation for Economic Education (FEE), which exposed me to numerous arguments for libertarianism in a life-changing and compelling way. I remember realizing for the first time that I had a strong argument for why education should be privatized. I remember learning about why monopoly power can only be truly granted by governments and not gained through market competition. The light bulbs started to go off, but I was reluctant to cast off my label as a conservative—so I decided that I was a conservative with libertarian sympathies.

My time as a student at Regent University continued to challenge my thinking—as well as an eventual summer internship at FEE in 2010. During this time, I realized that government ought to be limited to only the provision of defense—and maybe one or two other things (a position known as *minarchism*). I was ready to concede that I was a limited government libertarian, and by my senior year, I readily described myself as a minarchist. Exposure to the writings of St. Augustine, Alexis de Tocqueville, and the founding fathers only further deepened my distrust for political authority and propelled me to err on the side of individual liberty in the face of state power. I was blessed during this time with professors who allowed me to think independently but not lazily. None of my professors would likely self-identify as libertarians, but perhaps just as importantly, they were rigorous and open to a free exchange of well-argued ideas, which created a healthy environment for me to further consider these concepts.

It didn't take long for me to make a final leap from libertarian minarchism to *anarcho-capitalism,* the belief that state power is wholly illegitimate and can be ultimately replaced by market and other private forces (though the argument I make in this chapter will appeal to political thought across the libertarian spectrum). Shortly after I graduated college, I moved to Arlington, Virginia, just outside of Washington, DC, to start my first full-time job. To prepare for my living expenses, I diligently created a detailed budget before I even started receiving my salary. I was preparing to marry my fiancée, Leah (author of chapter 4), the following year and I wanted to aggressively save some money. I made one mistake in my budget though—I underestimated how much the federal and state governments were going to take away from me through withholding.

When I opened my first pay stub and saw how much I was paid compared to how much I took home after withholding, I was beyond livid. I realized that I needed to redo my budget and make some cuts, because the government was taking much more than I had anticipated. It was at that moment that I realized that I could not justify the government stealing anyone's money at any amount or percentage for any purpose. I realized that no one should have their money taken away from them before it was even deposited in their bank account. I admitted to myself that all compulsory taxation for any reason is, for all intents and purposes, theft—and I could not come up with an argument to institutionally legitimize it.

Since the state is funded by compulsory taxation, I also realized that I could not ideologically support its serving of any function, including the provision of police, defense, and legal courts. What if someone is a pacifist—should they be forced to pay for a military that violated their basic beliefs? What if an innocent individual is irreparably harmed by police during a drug raid? Why force that person to continue paying for police services? How could that be justified? There was no line to draw that made reasonable sense. Thus, my commitment to anarcho-capitalism was solidified—and it has only grown through further study and observation of the political climate in Washington, DC. Often, I feel like a Gondorian living across the river from Mordor.

And thus, here I am today: sixteen years removed from the 2000 election. I no longer care much about the political world of presidents, congressional leaders, Supreme Court appointees, etc. I also care little for elections and campaigns. I care far more about how to reduce the power of these individuals and the political institutions in which they operate in order to protect the lives, liberties, and properties of individuals against unjust violations. I do this as a Christian first and foremost and secondly as a libertarian. The past sixteen years have been a journey for me, a journey from devoted Republicanism and neoconservativism, to a deep distrust of the political system—and even more importantly, to a realization that the betterment of individual's lives happens much more frequently *outside of politics*. My wife, Leah, will address that topic in much deeper detail in chapter 5.

As for my forthcoming thoughts, I believe that it is not only possible to develop a libertarian perspective while maintaining a fervent belief in Christianity but that there's a strong case for such a perspective. Given the unfortunate and false perception that libertarianism is the political philosophy of drug addicts and polyamorous lovers, proving this assertion might seem a difficult task to the non-libertarian Christian. However, when we properly define libertarianism and then search the scriptures in their totality to learn what the Bible says about the institution of government, I think many Christians are in for a surprise.

THE QUESTION BEFORE US

There are two questions that Christians must ask when considering the proper role of government is according to scripture. Those questions are:

1. What does the Bible tell us about the role of government?

2. In light of what the Bible says about government, what should be our perspective on government?

It cannot be overstated that these questions pose a complex challenge. Each of us must honestly wrestle with the implications of our answers— there are no clean-cut solutions that we can learn in Sunday school on this topic. In fact, anyone who says that the answer to these questions is straightforward has probably not thoughtfully considered the relationship between the Christian faith and notions of political authority and obligation.

Furthermore, a fairly acute complication that presents itself as we try to answer these questions is that the Bible is not a work of political philosophy. The Bible is much grander than Plato's *Republic,* Aristotle's *Politics,* and John Locke's *Two Treatises of Government*—it tells us first and foremost about God and our relationship to him. But this is fundamentally not a thesis of political philosophy comparable to the theses we might read in Plato, Aristotle, and Locke.

On this point, Robert Kraynak, professor of political science at Colgate University, argues that Christians "must begin by acknowledging that

Christianity is an otherworldly religion whose primary mission is saving souls in the world-to-come rather than constructing political regimes . . . "[3] Kraynak's observation reminds us of the unchanging core of the Christian faith: the gospel of Christ. In contrast, political cultures and climates are ever changing according to the whims and fancies of the day. If we as Christians are to remain sound in their doctrine, then we must be careful not to make specific notions of temporal regimes and political authority integral to our faith. Thus, we must be careful in assuming that certain biblical texts have a fundamental meaning in the context of political philosophy—lest we risk imposing our political preferences on a text for the sake of advancing our pet beliefs.

This challenge is only more compounded by the fact that the Bible does not tell us much about political philosophy to structure a political regime around its teachings. For instance, the Bible does not tell us what the ideal political regime structure should be, whether representative democracy is morally superior to monarchy, what sort of constitutional limitations should be present in a republic, the origins of the state, or whether individual rights are positive or negative (or whether rights exist at all). In the sense that the Bible speaks of the ideal, it does not speak of earthly regimes but of God's kingdom, which is above and beyond all human political aspirations.

Most importantly, the Bible does not say that one's political theory or, more precisely, one's views on the role of government are tied to one's salvation—and this is a crucial observation. Too often, when conversations get heated, we easily find ourselves feeling malice or even anger toward other Christians who advance political positions that do not jive with ours. This holds as true for myself as for any of you who might be reading this book— and for that I have to ask forgiveness for the times I have allowed myself to become bitter on the basis of someone's differing political beliefs. We must always remember that, when engaging in political conversations, as important as they are, they are not ultimate issues that affect our salvation—and thus, should not be grounds for strife, rudeness, or malice toward fellow believers who are also covered by the blood of Christ. There are simply no scriptural grounds for such behavior.

The bottom line is this: I don't usually pick up my Bible to learn how to fix my car or how to build a computer. Similarly, I do not read my Bible in order to learn how to structure a government—and I do not think that

---

3. Kraynak, *Christian Faith and Modern Democracy*, 183.

other Christians should either. We ought to read the Bible with a *much* higher purpose in mind. We should read our Bible to learn about who God is, how wise he is, how good he is, and what he has done, is doing, and will do for the salvation of lost sinners. We should read it to learn about our sin natures and what it means to be transformed into a new person in Christ. We should read it to learn about God the Father, God the Son, and God the Holy Spirit. We should read it to learn of God's sovereign movement throughout the history of the Israelite nation, culminating in the fulfillment of deliverance through the earthly ministry of Jesus Christ. We should read it to learn of the early church and the power of the gospel, of which, like Paul, we should never be ashamed.[4]

In short, the Bible addresses the most important subjects one can ever imagine. By saying the Bible is not a work of political philosophy, its importance is not decreased in the context of this conversation or any conversation. In fact, we ought to consider its importance heightened. We must also be on guard against allowing political prejudices to guide our understanding of a book that has a purpose far and above the sustaining of any earthly regime.

The savvy reader will point out that I might be in danger of contradicting myself. How can I say the Bible doesn't tell us much about government and then proceed to a discussion of how Christians can reconcile biblical teachings with libertarianism? My answer is as follows:

1. Many Christians think the Bible has a lot to say about political philosophy, relying on a select few passages in scripture. It is important to address these passages and their common interpretations to see if those passages justify what many Christians think about political authority.

2. Even though it deals with earthly and finite regimes, political philosophy is nevertheless important for Christians to understand, especially in light of their faith. While the Christian faith might not be centered on a political philosophy, it certainly speaks truths that can help orient our approach to political philosophy. In trying to understand what the Bible says about government, I hope to avoid the error of making an exclusive claim that the Bible mandates a particular political philosophy. Instead, I hope it will help Christians orient their thinking about the role of government as they remain consistent with biblical theological truths.

4. Rom 1:16.

3. Lastly, the Bible does tell us about human nature (one of the most important topics we can understand). Government agents are human beings susceptible to the same human nature as everyone else (see Rule 2 later in this chapter). What the Bible tells us about human nature can certainly speak authoritatively to our understanding of government actors (and actors in any sector of society).

WHAT IS GOVERNMENT ANYWAY?

Before trying to answer these questions, we need to define "government" and "libertarianism." In my experience, many Christians, including pastors and theologians, fail to carefully define their terms when talking about the role of government and the ethics of political authority—and this leads to a lot of arbitrary reasoning. I shall seek to avoid that problem here by defining these terms.

Government (or a "state") is a political organization of individuals that is distinguished from all other social institutions by two characteristics: (1) its *territorial monopoly* over lawmaking and enforcement and (2) its ability to collect revenue through *compulsory taxation* for the provision of services. Economists Max Weber and Hans-Hermann Hoppe both identify these characteristics as being uniquely associated with governments (or "states").[5]

Let's break this definition down a bit more by understanding how these characteristics distinguish government from any other social institution.

Consider a church and the authorities it has over its congregation. More specifically, consider what powers a church *does not* possess over its congregation, and you will immediately see the difference between church and state. No church has the legitimate authority to lock up individuals in the pew rows who don't contribute to the church offering plate (thus no church has the power of *compulsory taxation*). No church has the legitimate authority to enforce laws against adultery in its neighborhood by locking up adulterers (thus no church has the power of *territorial monopoly*).

Likewise, consider businesses and the lack of power they have over customers. Absent a prior government intervention, no business can approach customers with an offer of service and then threaten to throw the potential customer in jail for refusing to pay for the service. Imagine if Apple salespeople were allowed to throw potential customers in a caged cell

---

5. Hoppe, *Democracy: The God That Failed*, 45; Weber, "Politics as a Vocation," 77.

for refusing to buy an iPhone in the mall. Or imagine if Domino's delivery drivers brought pizzas to your door (without you placing an order) and then demanded that you pay $200 for the pizza—even if you were lactose intolerant! Simply put, businesses don't have that power, and thus, businesses do not have the power of *compulsory taxation*. Additionally, businesses (absent special grants from the government itself) do not naturally have the power of *territorial monopoly* because they cannot decide that everyone in a given region has to use their product or use their product in a certain way. Apple can't threaten the citizens of the state of Washington with jail time if they use a Samsung Galaxy or if they use an iPhone to watch a Samsung Galaxy ad.

The comparisons continue if we evaluate nonprofit organizations. No nonprofit can jail or otherwise penalize a potential donor if the donor decides to withhold financial support to the nonprofit. No nonprofit can establish a rule in a specific state or county that all individuals, under penalty of fines and jail time, ought to volunteer a certain number of hours in support of the nonprofit's mission.

In contrast, government has the perceived legitimacy to do any or all of these things if they wish to do so. Governments can establish and enforce laws over a given territory while also maintaining the perceived legitimacy to mandate the collection of revenue from individuals within said territory (whether those individuals want to pay for the government's services or not). If someone truly believes that the government's services are not effective at achieving their stated goals, they may not opt out of paying for those services. Even worse, if someone is definitively and irreparably harmed by government services, they *still* cannot opt out of paying for those services. If they do, the government will threaten that individual with fines and jail time (ultimately enforceable with guns, handcuffs, flashbangs, jail cells, and SWAT teams). If an individual believes that a government's law is unjust or abusive, they cannot opt out of complying with that law without facing the same threats. What are the implications of this?

Governmental authority is inherently grounded on one principle: the threat of aggressive violence against individuals for noncompliant behavior. Let me be clear: I write this *purely as a descriptive observation*, not a normative criticism. Many libertarians make the mistake of asserting that government is inherently violent in order to advance a moral criticism. I do not do so here. Violence is not inherently wrong, as it is sometimes necessary in cases of self-defense, so this observation is not an a priori condemnation of government. For instance, violence is clearly justified in self-defense or the defense of others. A father has every right to use violence against a sexual predator who is assaulting his daughter. A woman has every right to violently defend herself from a rapist. A private gun owner, with a clear shot at an active shooter, has every right to injure or kill the active shooter. These examples clearly indicate that violence is not inherently wrong, and thus the libertarian critique of government cannot merely be that government is grounded in violence.

However, this does not change the reality of how the state operates. Everything a state does, it accomplishes as a social organization that enforces its mandates through the threat of violence against those who will not pay up or who refuse to obey. We are not talking about a benevolent institution that is filled with jolly Santas, toy-making elves, and woodland gnomes. We are not talking about a charity. We are not talking about a beacon of moral teaching. We are talking about an institution that is distinguished from all other social institutions by its ability to inflict violence upon its citizens (or "customers"). The specifics of what the state demands may fluctuate wildly or not at all—ultimately, what the government demands of us is inconsequential to understanding the defining characteristics that establish the mechanism for how the government rules.

For example, if someone proposes that the government ought to launch a military intervention in Syria, then they propose that the government force American citizens (under threats of jail time and fines) to pay for the cost of funding that intervention. If someone proposes that the government raise the minimum wage, then they propose that the government force American business owners (under threats of jail time and fines) to pay their employees at a certain wage. If someone proposes that the government bail out financial institutions after an economic crisis, then they propose that the government force Americans (under threats of jail time and fines) to pay for the bailing out of those institutions.

At this juncture, some might be slightly confused: how are fines and threats of jail time really threats of violence? Is the IRS really going to show up at someone's door and point guns at them if they fail to pay their taxes?

If this is your question, then take a minute to reflect on the case of Eric Garner. You should remember his name. If you do not, then run a quick Google search. Eric Garner lived in New York City and made his living by selling single cigarettes for cash. On July 17, 2014, he was approached by police officers who thought that he was selling cigarettes from packets which did not have the appropriate tax stamp (whether Garner was actually selling cigarettes at the time is not confirmed). What happened next is truly shocking, and perhaps one of the most upsetting things that one could watch. Cell phone video footage shows the officers assaulting Garner, without any physical provocation on Garner's part, holding him in a chokehold until he loses consciousness. The footage recorded Garner gasping the words, "I can't breathe."[6] He was later declared dead at the hospital.

What was Garner's crime? If you watch the video, he did absolutely nothing to indicate that he was threatening or dangerous—he did raise his voice a tad and ask that the officers let him alone but hardly anything worthy of a violent attack. Technically, he did make a living selling cigarettes without collecting sales taxes, which was against New York law (in fact, Garner had been arrested multiple times before for the same offense). In attempting to enforce that law, the police officers killed Garner and were later cleared by a grand jury.

Some might say this analysis oversimplifies the issue. Admittedly, there were certainly a lot of issues raised with the Garner incident around contemporary policing tactics, institutional racism, and restitution. However, the fact remains that Garner was approached by officers for a specific legal reason—and that reason was because they suspected Garner of not paying his sales taxes.

Garner's case is a profound example of how taxation ultimately is backed up by the threat to use violence in enforcement of the collection of taxation. We often do not see it because the state has done a fantastic job of masking its threats, and most people are pretty good at complying. But in rare moments, like the Garner case, we get to see how violent the state can be when an individual is suspected of a crime as simple as not paying taxes on cigarette sales. This is why Stephen Carter, a law professor at Yale, mentions Eric Garner as a warning of the coercive violence behind all laws. Carter consequently makes it a point to "always counsel my first-year students never to support a law they are not willing to kill to enforce."[7]

In light of the above, it is essential to understand government as a territorial monopoly with the power to issue compulsory taxation, because it helps us understand that government's authority is based on the ability to threaten and ultimately use violence against individuals in order to force compelled obedience. If one does not recognize this fact, Christian

6. The Guardian, "I Can't Breathe."

7. Carter, "Law Puts Us All in the Same Danger.

or non-Christian, they cannot have an honest conversation about political authority and political obligation, because they are talking about government in a way that is inconsistent with reality.

This definition further helps us understand another point about government. Governments are run by men and women, individuals with the same basic passions, impulses, psychological issues, cognitive biases, and sinful temptations as the rest of us. They are not a special class of human beings who are immune from feelings of lust, envy, and hatred. They are not exempt from the constraints imposed by trade-offs or the physical realities of time and space. They also are not immune from abusing their authority, given their status, fame, and perceived legitimacy.

Again, this is a descriptive observation—all individuals in other settings or institutions might suffer from similar temptations and constraints. However, elected officials, judges, police officers, and bureaucrats do not make their careers in those other settings and institutions—they operate within an institution that allows them to use violence in order to enforce laws. There is simply no reason to believe that, in the enforcement of those laws, government actors possess special abilities that allow them to act outside of human nature or under a different set of moral rules than anyone else. French economist Frederic Bastiat pointed this out in 1850, noting that if political leaders thought they deserved such special exemptions from basic human nature, then the burden of proof rests on them to demonstrate their superiority and higher moral status.[8]

The last implication of this definition of government is that, descriptively speaking, governments tend to centralize their power over time. The rate of centralization is irrelevant to understanding this point. With sinful individuals at the helm of an organization tasked with ruling society, a guaranteed monopoly of lawmaking and guaranteed revenue from tax collection, there is no practical check that can stave off the centralization of political authority in government over the long run.[9] There may be short-term factors that work against centralizing forces in specific ways, but over the course of time, these short-term factors will be eroded by the incentives of governments, given their characteristics.

Again, this is a descriptive observation, not a moral condemnation. The entire history of the United States government, from a very limited constitutional republic in the late eighteenth century to an enormous

8. Bastiat, *The Law*, 46.
9. Hoppe, *Democracy, The God That Failed*, 82.

Progressivist leviathan today is arguably the best proof that governments will inevitably grow in power over time.[10] In a government that was *designed* to be severely limited in authority and function, power has still accumulated to frighteningly large degrees—and it has been happening for well over one hundred years at this point.

One need look no further than the twentieth century to understand the logical conclusion of government centralization. Political scientist, R.J. Rummel, calculates that roughly 262 million people were killed by their own governments in the twentieth century alone.[11] That statistic also excludes those who were killed fighting in the wars of the twentieth century. Consequently, Rummel's observations lead him to somewhat modify Lord Acton's famous dictum: "Power kills. Absolute power kills absolutely."[12] It goes without saying that churches, businesses, nonprofits, and other organizations have committed some terrible evils over the last century, but murdering 262 million people does not make their list of sins. Only governments have been able to accomplish such an impressive feat of wholesale brutality.

Admittedly, the 262 million individuals who were murdered by their own governments were murdered by totalitarian regimes—and the United States is far from a totalitarian regime. However, if one simply dismisses this statistic as a relic of Hitler's Germany, Stalin's Russia, and Pol Pot's Cambodia, concluding that the United States is a much better form of government, then the larger point has been missed. The point is that governments tend toward power, far more than any other social institution—and that power has inflicted far more damage upon the human race than any other social institution.

Thus, I make my first normative statement in light of the definition of government that I have here advanced: as Christians who do not want to see innocent lives murdered, punished, or abused, we must be extremely wary of adding powers to a social institution that has proven to be so dangerous throughout the totality of human civilization.

It is at this juncture that libertarianism begins to make its appeal to a Christian audience.

---

10. Ibid., 242–244.

11. Rummel, "20th Century Democide."

12. Rummel, *Power Kills*, 9.

WHAT IS LIBERTARIANISM?

Libertarianism is a political philosophy that is "concerned solely with the proper use of force. Its core premise is that it should be illegal to threaten or initiate violence against a person or his property without his permission; force is justified only in defense or retaliation."[13] In a word, the core of libertarianism is simply the idea that one person should not use violence against another person, with very few exceptions (namely self-defense). In conversation, many libertarians refer to this idea as the nonaggression principle, and it has been defended under both natural rights and utilitarian frameworks.

In his farewell address to Congress, former congressman Ron Paul encapsulated the libertarian response to the reality of state-sponsored violence, arguing that "to develop a truly free society, the issue of initiating force must be understood and rejected. Granting to government even a small amount of force is a dangerous concession."[14] It is interesting that, as an elected government official, Paul was so adamant about restricting the power of government. Perhaps he found himself tired of seeing how the sausage of law and legislation is made in Washington, DC.

As a political philosophy, libertarianism offers a normative response to the factual realities of state power. As the previous section demonstrated, government is backed up by the threat of violence, which includes the ability to send the police to one's home or business and forcibly demand obedience or payment in accordance with its mandates. The libertarian responds to this fact by saying that government ought to severely minimize, if not eliminate altogether, those threats of violence by the state. Otherwise, the government risks perpetuating injustice by using violence in an improper way by threatening and ultimately harming individuals who do not deserve to be treated violently.

There are a few implications from this definition of libertarianism. First, libertarianism does not celebrate personal and voluntary decisions to engage in moral deviancy. It might not argue for the legal punishment of such deviancy, but no libertarian is committed to supporting moral deviancy as a part of his ethical system. The libertarian is merely committed to not using aggressive force against an individual, even if he disagrees with that individual regarding personal morality. For more on this issue,

13. Block, "Libertarianism vs. Libertinism."
14. Paul, "Transcript of Farewell Address,"

see Taylor Barkley's chapter on the differences between libertarianism and libertinism.

Second, libertarianism does not attempt to explain how the world works—only to make ethical sense of what we know about how the political world works. The observation that government is a social apparatus backed by the threat of violence is not a libertarian observation (i.e. one does not need to be a libertarian to agree with that assessment, although libertarians may be more inclined to be aware of that reality than socialists, progressives, or conservatives). The libertarian evaluates the reality of government as a social apparatus of force and concludes that such power is potentially dangerous and ought to be vastly limited, if not eliminated. The moral problems of humans wielding authority over others, backed by constant threats of violence, pose too many risks to life, health, and well-being (a utilitarian perspective) or violate fundamental rights (a natural rights perspective) to allow for an even mildly powerful government.

Thirdly and finally, libertarianism does not advance any propositions about the nature of God, salvation, or human nature. A libertarian may believe in God, or he or she may not. A libertarian may believe that human nature is depraved, or he or she may believe that human nature is naturally good. A libertarian may believe that Jesus Christ is the Son of God, or he or she may not. These views are held independent of one's libertarianism—which is why this book argues for the *compatibility* of libertarianism and Christianity, not the inherent connection.

That said, I personally believe that my Christian faith significantly strengthens my libertarianism because of the ethical, theological, and philosophical commitments I make as a Christian. Without the ethical framework provided by the triune God of Christianity, I (personally) cannot make a morally convincing case for libertarianism. Without the Christian doctrine of human sin, I am at a loss to explain the constant and inordinate injustices perpetuated by political rulers throughout history. And without the Christian doctrine of the Imago Dei, I have a much harder time arguing for the inherent worth and dignity of the individual in the face of abusive authority.

LAYING THE GROUND RULES

At this juncture, it is important to mention something about the burden of proof in this chapter. This chapter will argue that libertarianism and Christianity, based on the Bible's teachings, are compatible with each other. However,

45

it does not follow from this claim that I have to prove that *all* strands of libertarianism are necessarily compatible with Christianity, only that *mere* libertarianism is compatible with *mere* Christianity. There are many interpretations of libertarian thought, with various claims ranging from interesting to outrageous. In reality, many of these claims are not germane to the core of libertarianism as defined at the outset of this chapter—and thus do not disprove the thesis. Libertines, Objectivists, and atheist libertarians who hold that a belief in God is incompatible with liberty are good examples of perspectives within libertarianism that I am not defending here today.

To hold both myself and my readers accountable as we assess the case for the compatibility of libertarianism and Christianity, we must follow several rules in order to avoid sloppy thinking. These rules are designed to help us avoid contradicting basic and fundamental Christian doctrines when we venture into the realm of political thought as Christians. They are also meant to help us avoid basic logical fallacies. In so doing, these rules should provide a general framework that Christians can agree with when discussing the issues at hand. These rules do not slant us inherently toward libertarianism or any other ideology. Rather, they protect us from poor habits of thought and doctrinal error as we foray into the world of political ideology.

Rule 1: As Christians, we must assume that God is, *prima facie*, worthy of greater worship and obedience than any government or political leader (or any other human being or aspect of creation). If we are to agree with the Psalmist who wrote, "For great is the Lord, and greatly to be praised; he is to be feared above all gods,"[15] or with the first commandment itself,[16] then we must not advance an argument for political authority that ascribes sovereignty, praise, or worship that should only belong to God. If we do advance such an argument, then we implicitly admit that human political authority can be at least equivalent, if not superior, to God's authority. For Christians, it should go without saying that pledging allegiance to Jesus is far superior to pledging allegiance to the flag or celebrating Ronald Reagan or Barack Obama.

Rule 2: We may not assume that government actors are fundamentally different in terms of their human nature from other human beings. Romans 3:23 tells us that "all have sinned and fall short of the glory of

---

15. Ps 96:4
16. Exod 20:3

God."[17] This verse applies equally to all human beings, whether they possess political authority or not. Thus, we cannot advance an argument in favor of political authority that assumes a higher level of benevolence, love, or charity than we can expect from human beings with a sin nature. We also cannot advance an argument that ignores the effects of that sin nature on political authorities. As Michael Huemer, philosophy professor at the University of Colorado Boulder, observes, "One can design social institutions on the assumption that people are unselfish, but this will not cause people to be unselfish; it will simply cause those institutions to fail."[18]

Rule 3: We must avoid "moral chaos" bias. By that, I mean, we must resist the urge to see contemporary moral failings as evidence of an ever-declining Western civilization. We ought not to presume that moral theory is on the decline for two reasons: first, because the contemporary moral failings that we observe are by no means unique to our time and culture and, second, because general moral theories among the common man are arguably improved relative to past cultures.

As Huemer argues, modern moral attitudes shaped by contemporary philosophical perspectives are culturally superior to the moral attitudes accepted by humans in the ancient and medieval world. Gladiator games, slavery, child sacrifice, sawing insubordinate prisoners in half, cooking people alive, burning heretics and witches at the stake, and raping an entire female population of a town or city are universally derided today, but were often generally accepted—and practiced—by our ancestors.[19] These are no slight moral and cultural improvements, yet they are often overlooked whenever we complain about contemporary matters of "cultural decay." This does not mean that all contemporary moral theory is perfectly good or that there are not significant moral failings remaining in society (abortion being at the forefront of such failings), but we must be realistic about assessing and comparing moral theories over time rather than myopically catastrophizing present day issues. This is especially the case when we consider the role of government as Christians—if we start from a position of moral chaos bias, we are more likely to be less rational in assessing political considerations, allowing the whims of politics to carry us to and fro as we attempt to assuage our fears about "moral failure" through the political system. Note that I do not say we should ignore significant and contemporary

17. Rom. 3:33
18. Huemer, *The Problem of Political Authority*, 242.
19. Ibid., 323–324.

moral failures, only that we must not allow such failures to lead us to hasty conclusions about the future degradation of Western civilization.

Most importantly, as Christians, we should be at the forefront of celebrating improvements of moral and political theories when they help realize a greater respect for the dignity of the individual and the improvement of the soul. Moral chaos bias often does not allow Christians to see these improvements for what they are since they are constantly looking for contemporary problems in moral sentiments and theories rather than for improvements. In reality, Christians ought to realize that the ancient wisdom in the Bible provides us with some of the most powerful arguments for accepting and celebrating a modern improvement in moral and political philosophy relative to eras when horrible and abusive practices were accepted as normal both by elites and the common man.

Rule 4: We must avoid proof-texting, or in other words, justifying our opinions on complex topics based on the words of a few specific scripture verses (Jacqueline Isaacs discusses this issue in her chapter as well). We may not assume that individual scripture passages are sufficient to refute, support, or otherwise speak to an established argument in economics or political philosophy. Some might read this as a refutation of the authority of scripture over human knowledge—and they would be wrong.

Quite simply, Christians should not engage in lazy thinking and the misuse of scripture to justify personal opinions. If a scholar advocates an argument for the role of government, grounded in hundreds of years of political discourse, philosophical tradition, and ethical inquiry, it is not enough to throw out a reference to Romans 13 or the Beatitudes by way of response. Lobbing a Bible verse into the air whenever we confront an uncomfortable argument from political philosophy or economics is not a sufficient substitute for considering the argument on its own merit. We must think with a biblical framework, but we must not use the Bible to excuse poorly formed opinions based on isolated readings of specific passages. If anything, this brings disgrace to the testimony and power of scripture.

Rule 5: We may not assume that American constitutionalism is a biblically mandated or biblically supported form of government. This rule is supported by the scholar, Robert Kraynak, who calls the current acceptance of democratic politics among Christian theologians, pastors, and congregations, "a historical anomaly, a peculiarity of modern times."[20] Kraynak

---

20. Kraynak, *Christian Faith and Modern Democracy*, 3.

further contends that much of the Christian tradition is "rather illiberal and undemocratic for much of its history."[21]

This might be a difficult pill for some to swallow. However, the Bible nowhere outlines the American system of government as God's gift to the world in the way that many American Christians speak of it. The Bible does not argue for a system of limited and enumerated powers with constitutional checks and balances—we find much more relevant information regarding these topics in the writings of Locke, Madison, Montesquieu, and others. The Bible does not tell us to establish an executive, legislative, and judicial branch. Most pertinently, much of the Bible was written thousands of years before the idea of the American Constitution was even conceived. The authors of the New Testament were more focused on the coming of Jesus Christ than the coming of James Madison.

Of course, a rigorous historical analysis will show that most of the men who contributed in significant ways to the founding of the United States were either committed Christians (Patrick Henry, Samuel Adams, and John Jay) or Deists (such as Thomas Paine, Benjamin Franklin, and Thomas Jefferson). They either believed in the triune God of the Bible or were influenced by that belief, even if they did not accept it. However, this does not mean that the American system of government is a Christian notion of government.

With these rules in mind, we can proceed to analyze the question at hand.

WHAT DOES THE BIBLE SAY ABOUT GOVERNMENT?

Five Biblical Themes

At long last, we have arrived: what does the Bible say about government? In order to avoid proof-texting, I want to begin this section by establishing five major *themes* about government, pulling from a fairly extensive list of passages in scripture. After these themes are addressed, I will move on to some specific passages that may have already come to your mind, including Romans 13, First Peter 2, and both gospel accounts of Christ's statement to "render unto Caesar" in Matthew and Luke.

It is important to consider these more popular passages about government in light of the rest of scripture, specifically when scripture speaks to

21. Ibid.

the subject of rulers and authority. Although cited often, Romans 13, First Peter 2, and the "render unto Caesar" passages are not the only passages that speak of government authority and the power to rule. There are others that should give Christians much greater pause when considering whether to legitimize political authority or to advocate obedience to political rulers. They include the following passages:

Acts 5:27–29

1 Samuel 8

2 Samuel 12:1–13

Ecclesiastes 4:1–3

Psalm 2:1–6

Psalm 22:28

Psalm 146:3

Mark 10:42–45

John 18:36

I encourage you to read these passages in full. I will cite these passages specifically as I go, allowing you to see how they fit into the overall argument. These themes articulate a biblical perspective of government that is far less rosy than the mainstream Christian perspective on government that we discussed and further support the view that Christians ought to be highly wary of sword-wielding humans in the office of government.

Theme 1: Government Is Filled with Sinful Humans.

This is the first theme that emerges from these passages—and it should be one of the most obvious points for any Christian to accept. In Psalm 2:1–6, David describes the folly and wickedness of kings who set themselves up in opposition to God and observes how God laughs at them and "holds them in derision."[22] It's clear these kings and rulers are sinners and God-haters who are unworthy in the face of God's justice. David, himself a great sinner

22. Ps 2:2–4: "The kings of the earth set themselves, and the rulers take counsel together, against the Lord and against his Anointed, saying, 'Let us burst their bonds apart and cast away their cords from us.' He who sits in the heavens laughs; the Lord holds them in derision."

as Israel's king, expresses his feelings toward these kings through righteous anger at their wicked desires.

In Ecclesiastes 4 (the first verse is quoted at the beginning of this chapter), the tone of criticism switches from righteous anger to grief over the sinfulness of rulers. David's son Solomon grieves over the tears of the oppressed and notes that on the side of their oppressors is power. As a result of that power, there is no place for the oppressed to turn for reprieve or rightful restoration. He concludes the first verse by reiterating his grief that there is no one to comfort the oppressed.[23] When we consider the 262 million victims of government-sponsored murder in the twentieth century, we realize the depth and power of Solomon's grief. When we consider the specific cases of individuals like Eric Garner, we have a chance to share in that grief as we stare into the face of a victim of political authority.

Lastly, in Psalm 146:3,[24] we see a warning against placing one's trust in princes. The psalmist is clear to emphasize the mortality of rulers and, by extension, emphasizes their sinfulness. According to Christian doctrine, all mortals struggle with their own sin natures and all are touched by the realities of sin's corrupting influence. It's no small matter that the psalmist emphasizes this when encouraging his audience not to place their trust in princes. Of course, we know who the psalmist does believe we should put our faith in and in whom resides the power of salvation. This leads to the second theme.

Theme 2: God Is Greater Than Any Political Authority.

As obvious as the first theme should be to Christians, this theme should be equally so—and it comes through in the following passages. Psalm 22:28 says that "kingship belongs to the Lord, and he rules over the nations."[25] No king, no president, and no prime minister has any authority or power that is outside of God's sovereignty. No legislative mandate or court ruling is exempt from God's standard for justice. No police officer or soldier can morally put himself or herself in the place of God when choosing to enforce the laws of their country. If police officers or soldiers do, they will someday have to answer to God for how they used their power. If someone cares

23. Eccl 4:1

24. Ps 146:3: "Put not your trust in princes, in a son of man, in whom there is no salvation."

25. Ps 22:28

enough about politics to even run for political office, they should honestly be petrified of the very power they seek. With just a few bad incentives, poor policies, and corrupt enforcers and successors, the political power that one might think is used for good today can quickly become a weapon against the innocent tomorrow. This has great significance to the Christian's view of government: we ought to be aware of and critical of political authorities who command obedience of their subjects, especially when such commands of obedience results in the Christian either directly engaging in or supporting evil practices.

On a related note, but still on the same theme, this recognition of God's greatness over earthly political authority means Christians have an obligation to always seek to obey God first rather than men. All political authority must be scrutinized as a human authority first and then considered in light of our ethical commitments to God. When Peter was commanded to cease preaching the gospel of Christ in Acts 5, he responded by saying, "We must obey God rather than men."[26] The inherent worthiness of God compared to the general unworthiness of human political authorities makes it a logical decision for a Christian to follow their conscience and make the right moral decisions even in the midst of a trying political climate.

Theme 3: Political Power Tends to Corrupt the Wielder of Power.

Look no further than Samuel's grave warnings to the Israelites when they asked for a king. When Israel demanded a king, the Lord told Samuel to relay a warning to the people about how corrupt and abusive this king would become. As a result, Samuel told the people about all the things that the king would do to them. He told them that the king would conscript their sons into his army and that he would take their daughters and force them to be his perfumers and bakers. He also warned that the king would take the *best* of their fields and vineyards and gift them to his loyal officers—a clear example of cronyism. He continues to warn about all of the things that the king will take from the people of Israel and finally concludes his warning by saying, "and you shall be his slaves. And in that day you will cry out because of your king, whom you have chosen for yourselves, but the Lord will not answer you in that day."[27]

26. Acts 5:39
27. 1 Sam 8:18

Needless to say, Samuel's warnings were not idle threats. It didn't take long for Israel's first king, Saul, to find himself corrupted by his power. Even King David, the man after God's own heart, and his son Solomon, the builder of God's holy temple, fell prey to the temptations of power in their various ways. And of course, after them came a long list of kings, many of whom did "evil in the eyes of the Lord" (See 1 Kings 21:25, 2 Kings 13:2, and 2 Kings 16:2 for a few examples).

On the flip side of the corrupting power of political authority, we find Jesus talking to his disciples in the Gospel of Mark about what it means to be great. He starts by telling them, "You know that those who are considered rulers of the Gentiles lord it over them, and their great ones exercise authority over them."[28] In contrast to the example of the Gentile rulers, Christ says to his disciples, "But it shall not be so among you. But whoever would be great among you must be your servant, and whoever would be first among you must be slave of all. For even the Son of Man came not to be served but to serve, and to give his life as a ransom for many."[29]

This is really something! Christ specifically tells his disciples that they will not be recognized for their greatness by the authority that they wield over others, but instead for how they serve one another. And then he punctuates this point by telling his disciples that he is the ultimate example of this principle. The Christian call to humbly serve others trumps the call to wield political authority.

Is it possible that someone who possesses political authority might not be corrupted by a lust for power or the thrill of political successes and the personal benefits thereby accrued? I'll grant that it is possible. But is it likely, given the institutional structure of government and human nature? No, it is not. And moreover, it is very risky to structure a government on the basis of hoping a few individuals will not be corrupted in the midst of a sea of corruption.

Theme 4: Christians Ought to Grieve over the Abuse of Power.

Returning to Ecclesiastes 4, you can practically hear the grief-stricken anguish in the writing. The oppressed have nowhere to turn and no one to comfort them. Nothing stands in the way of the powerful abusers.

---

28. Mark 10:42
29. Mark 10:43–45

I really think this is where most modern Christians slip up, especially in the United States. We are far too eager to not only ignore the problems of the oppressed but, in some cases, to even celebrate their oppressors. For example, in 2014, Christian evangelist Franklin Graham did this when he posted on his Facebook page about the issue of police brutality, attributing the recent wave of deaths at the hands of law enforcement to the disobedience of the alleged criminals. He said,

> Listen up—Blacks, Whites, Latinos, and everybody else. Most police shootings can be avoided. It comes down to respect for authority and obedience. If a police officer tells you to stop, you stop. If a police officer tells you to put your hands in the air, you put your hands in the air. If a police officer tells you to lay down face first with your hands behind your back, you lay down face first with your hands behind your back. It's as simple as that. Even if you think the police officer is wrong—you obey. Parents, teach your children to respect and obey those in authority. Mr. President, this is a message our nation needs to hear, and they need to hear it from you. Some of the unnecessary shootings we have seen recently might have been avoided. The Bible says to submit to your leaders and those in authority "because they keep watch over you as those who must give an account."[30]

Graham and the roughly two hundred thousand people who liked his comment forgot something very important: they not only simplified a complex issue but did so in a way that praised the authorities with power while failing to express a whiff of sentiment for anyone who has been unjustly murdered at the hands of police. Instead of beating the drum of obedience to unjust authority, I believe that Graham should have behaved more like the prophet Nathan in 2 Samuel 12:1–13. Nathan was both grieved and righteously angered over David's sin, which notably involved a gross abuse of his power, and called him out for it. Nathan did not care that David was the king of Israel who possessed political power. If only Franklin Graham and his followers had the courage to do the same when the opportunity arose to confront and call out abusive police officers. Biblically speaking, abuse should evoke grief, not blind loyalty to the source of abuse.

---

30. Graham's Facebook page.

Theme 5: Christianity Is Advanced through the Gospel of Christ, Not Political Authority or Obedience to It.

When Christ was asked by Pontius Pilate if he claimed to be the king of the Jews, Christ responded, "My kingdom is not of this world. If my kingdom were of this world, my servants would have been fighting, that I might not be delivered over to the Jews. But my kingdom is not from the world."[31]

Christ not only says it once; he says it twice: "My kingdom is not of this world." The implication for believers is that Christ's kingdom is better and above any kingdom of this world. The city of God beats the city of man every time. The city of man is corrupt, sinful, and abusive. It is not worth worshipping, and many times, it's not even really worth obeying unless one is trying to avoid the violence that political authorities wield against disobedient subjects.

How do we advance God's kingdom? Is it by electing candidates, driving public policy debates, or picketing in front of the Supreme Court? There's little reason to think that there is, and for those who disagree, reconsider the words of Christ in response to Pontius Pilate. I do not mean to suggest that political activism is unbiblical, and while I can understand why many are quick to view it as a primary avenue for social change, count me a skeptic *on biblical grounds*. If Christ's kingdom *truly* is not of this world, then trying to tie our identities, values, and beliefs to political parties or legislative policies is trying to marry two things that don't mix very well. It can potentially damage our witness as Christians, especially when we choose hypocritical candidates or bad legislation with harmful unintended consequences to the poor and the vulnerable.

Romans 13 and First Peter 2

These themes will be important to remember as we move forward into a discussion of what I call the "Big Four." Romans 13, First Peter 2, Matthew 22, and Luke 20 are *widely* referred to in Christian circles when discussing the idea of whether or not government is legitimate and what our obedience to it should look like.

Moreover, I have chosen to address these four passages in scripture because they represent potentially the most concerning obstacle to being both a Christian and a libertarian as I have defined libertarianism. These

31. John 18:36

passages seem to imply that government authority is divinely supported by God himself and that individuals therefore must obey government's laws and pay whatever taxes it requires.

In contrast, the libertarian position is that government is a human institution and is not of divine inspiration. Moreover, libertarians have a much larger respect for civil disobedience in the face of unjust law, even if the law has nothing to do with the violation of one's duties toward God. Although many non-religious libertarians will easily dismiss these passages since they reject scriptural authority in the first place, libertarian Christians must grapple with them to remain consistent in both their faith and their libertarianism.

The first passage to consider is in Romans 13, from verses 1–7.

> Let every person be subject to the governing authorities. For there is no authority except from God, and those that exist have been instituted by God. Therefore whoever resists the authorities resists what God has appointed, and those who resist will incur judgment. For rulers are not a terror to good conduct, but to bad. Would you have no fear of the one who is in authority? Then do what is good, and you will receive his approval, for he is God's servant for your good. But if you do wrong, be afraid, for he does not bear the sword in vain. For he is the servant of God, an avenger who carries out God's wrath on the wrongdoer. Therefore one must be in subjection, not only to avoid God's wrath but also for the sake of conscience. For because of this you also pay taxes, for the authorities are ministers of God, attending to this very thing. Pay to all what is owed to them: taxes to whom taxes are owed, revenue to whom revenue is owed, respect to whom respect is owed, honor to whom honor is owed.

Here, Paul seems to provide both an explanation of where political authority comes from and why political authority ought to be obeyed. Furthermore, Paul seems to argue that the Christian possesses a duty to obey political authority, specifically saying there is "no authority except from God." Paul goes on further to say that resisting the authorities that God has appointed will incur judgment, a sentiment that gives a libertarian Christian reason to pause. And finally, after equating the actions of political rulers with the judgments of God (a bearer of the sword and avenger of God's wrath against the wrongdoer and a rewarder of the righteous), Paul tells his audience to pay taxes, revenue, respect, and honor to whom it is owed.

How can this be consistent with libertarianism, which has a hard time even justifying the state's existence, let alone advocating for submission and the payment of taxes?

The issue in interpreting this text comes down to two points: the concept of authority to which Paul refers and the historical context within which Paul was writing. If Paul's conception of authority refers to the idea of government as defined earlier in this chapter with the exclusive characteristics of taxation and a territorial legal monopoly, then the libertarian Christian faces a potential challenge in opposing government, viewing it as inherently illegitimate or seeking to drastically reduce its power. If that government holds its authority from God and if that government does not bear the sword in vain, then resisting it is not only disobedient to that government, but to God himself. Thus, we must attempt to clarify what Paul meant when he mentioned authority.

Furthermore, if Paul was writing this as a statement of Christian political philosophy (and authority is taken to include government) that is binding across generations, cultures, and governments, then the libertarian Christian also faces a serious challenge. Was Paul writing Romans 13 as a literal command to not only the Roman church, but to Christians throughout time? Or was he writing specifically regarding the issue of political submission to Roman authorities due to the political climate in Rome? Did he actually intend to describe God's role for government or did he have more contextually specific meanings for phrases such as "the servant of God, an avenger who carries out God's wrath?" Ultimately, when it comes to interpretation, we ought to determine whether Romans 13 should be interpreted *literally* as a binding command for all Christians or as a *historically contextual exhortation to the Christians in Rome*. Ultimately, the latter has favorable implications for the libertarian Christian although a literal interpretation is not terribly problematic, as I will hereafter demonstrate.

Thus, how to interpret Romans 13 in the context of considering libertarianism boils down to the following:

1. Should Romans 13 be interpreted *literally* as a binding command for all Christians or as a *historically contextual exhortation* to the Christians in Rome?

2. If Romans 13 is to be interpreted *literally* as a binding command for all Christians, then what did Paul mean when he referred to authority?

3. If Romans 13 is to be interpreted as a *historically contextual exhortation*, what is the applicability of Romans 13 to Christians who engage in political philosophy in a modern context?

To start, let us consider the first two questions. Let us assume that Paul wrote Romans 13 as an absolute command that transcends specific political and cultural circumstances and has binding significance for all Christians. Is it still possible to be a libertarian Christian? who views the state merely as a necessarily evil—or perhaps even illegitimate?

In short, yes. Paul almost certainly did not have a modern conception of the state (as defined by Weber and Hoppe) when he used the word, "authority," which in the original Greek was *exousia*. Strong's Concordance defines *exousia* as "(in the sense of ability); privilege, i.e. (subjectively) force, capacity, competency, freedom, or (objectively) mastery (concretely, magistrate, superhuman, potentate, token of control), delegated influence: —authority, jurisdiction, liberty, power, right, strength."[32]

While political authorities at the helm of a state apparatus may embody some of these characteristics, it does not follow that these characteristics are exclusive to political authorities—or even that political authorities truly can lay claim to this conception of authority. It is quite possible that Paul is speaking of a broader conception of authority that includes other notions of authority which can embody these characteristics, whether spiritual authority, church authority, familial authority, managerial authority, or other notions of authority. This is a crucial point for a Christian consideration of libertarianism. If Paul's comments in praise of authority are not exclusive to political authority, then rightful authority could logically come from sources outside of politics—and potentially have more legitimate claims to authority than their political counterparts.

It is important that Christians understand that the modern state is a creation of man, and thus, it is not likely to be around forever. Perhaps it may remain for a long time, but that does not make it a good or justified form of authority. Speaking hypothetically, if better systems of authority could emerge where the ability to aggress against innocent individuals was not included as a measure of authority, then it hardly seems unchristian or antibiblical to desire those better systems of authority. Political authority in the status quo, even in the United States, is based on the political elite's ability to coerce and command, extort tribute through tax policy, and selectively

32. Strong, *Strong's Exhaustive Concordance*, G1849.

58

apply laws to others but not themselves. Not only is this obviously not the best system of human authority, it can be safely and reasonably argued that the political authority we see today might not even be legitimate at all.[33] It does not seem that we would be outside the bounds of Romans 13 by seeking out or desiring a contractually based system of authority that does not rest upon aggression, in agreement with the ethos of the libertarian. We would simply be opting for a better form of authority than the status quo.

Therefore, in practical terms, even if we assume that Romans 13 is a binding mandate for Christians throughout time, it is highly unlikely that Paul was thinking only of submitting to the state with its defining characteristics.

Furthermore, Paul only speaks of just authorities in this passage—authorities that punish the evildoer and reward the righteous. He does not consider evil authorities who command things like the murder of all children in a conquered village. He does not address rulers who enslave entire nations and allows their soldiers to rape female captives. He does not address kings, princes, pharaohs, or Caesars who persecute God's children. Thus, if this passage is to be interpreted as *a binding command with normative import* for the Christian, it must be considered as such only because Paul speaks of submitting to *just* authority.

But what about taxes? This does seem to apply to the definition of government presented earlier in this chapter, and Paul does clearly seem to say that Christians should pay their taxes. However, Paul does not say that taxes ought to be paid with an unqualified statement. He says taxes, along with honor and respect, are to be paid *to whom they are due*. This is an interesting qualification because it forces us to ask: who deserves to receive taxes, honor, and respect?

Paul seems to answer this in the preceding verses, arguing that the authorities of God who do not bear the sword in vain will bring God's wrath against the wrongdoer. The authority who deserves taxes also gives approval to the righteous. For the sake of argument, let's assume that each reference to authority *is* a reference exclusively to political authority in the context of the state. Even if that is the interpretative position one wishes to take, we quickly realize that very few political authorities deserve to be respected and obeyed by the very guidelines that Paul establishes here. The history of governments has been one of violence against both subjects and foreigners—a nasty and brutish state of war against each other and against individuals. When one realizes how strict the criteria here are for political

---

33. Huemer, *The Problem of Political Authority*, 334.

authority (if we are to interpret authority in a purely political context), agents of the state become quickly undeserving of the honor, respect, tribute, and taxes that we are alleged to owe them. This reference to taxation in the context of the phrase "to whom they are due" reinforces the notion that Paul is exhorting Christians to submit to just authority as the normative principle of our literal interpretation.

Clearly, in answering the first two questions, there is no reason for a libertarian Christian to fret. The concept of authority that Paul refers to here does not necessarily mean political authority, and even if it did, then Paul only exhorts Christians to submit to just political authority. This only presents a problem for a Christian anarcho-capitalist who does not believe in the legitimacy of political authority at all. However, in a broad sense, libertarian Christians who do not accept anarcho-capitalism but instead prefer a highly minimal state have little to fear from a literal interpretation of Romans 13 so long as we take care to understand the various notions of authority to which Paul might be referring in this passage.

At this juncture, it is important to consider the third question above: is the scope of Romans 13 actually intended for an audience of Christians beyond the church in Rome? Should it actually have a high degree of import when governing our thinking on political philosophy? Essentially, should we ignore the literal interpretation, even with the understanding that it might refer to many different types of authority and opt for a more contextually based interpretation?

The answer is that there is good reason to actually reject the binding interpretation of Romans 13 and actually view it as a specific exhortation within a given political climate. Its applicability beyond that in helping us to understand the ideals of political philosophy may actually be a misuse of the passage as it was intended. New Testament scholar Marcus Borg argues that Paul wrote Romans 13 under the context of the specific political climate of the Roman Empire and the many rumblings of revolution, zealotry, and nationalism associated with those who were frustrated with its rule. Borg chronicles a number of historical events from contemporary historians, including Josephus and Seutonius, noting that the Jewish community in Rome likely had strong anti-Roman sentiments and that this would have had an effect on the early church in Rome, especially for those Christians who had a Jewish heritage.[34] Borg thus contends that "Paul's famous generalizations about governing authorities were intended, not as abiding prin-

---

34. Borg, "A New Context for Romans XIII," 209–214.

ciples to be applied in every situation, but as specific advice to particular people facing a historically identifiable set of circumstances."[35]

Borg further notes that much textual evidence exists, both in Romans 12 and Romans 13, to support the idea that Paul did not mean this passage as a definitive statement of Christian political philosophy regarding all institutions of civil government—or as a binding command for all Christians. Rather, Borg believes that Paul saw the Roman government as a specific tool of God's judgment in the same way that prophets like Isaiah, Jeremiah, and Ezekiel saw when they warned of the pagan governments in Babylon and Assyria who God also used to execute his wrath in specific historical circumstances.[36] This would explain Paul's comment about authority (interpreted as Roman political authority) as an agent of God's wrath—in the same way that the Old Testament prophets warned of other pagan empires as agents of God's wrath. Given Paul's extensive scholarly background, he would have been more than familiar with the concept of God using pagan governments as vessels of judgment.

Similarly, Borg analyzes the phrase, "he is God's servant for your good," noting this was likely a reference to the Roman Christians' ultimate good of salvation, not a reference to their good as civil subjects or humans with individual rights. In the context of the rest of Romans, especially Romans 12, Borg believes that it makes sense that Paul was encouraging the Roman Christians amid a time of political turbulence and the possibility of antigovernment uprisings to remember to endure the evils of this world and focus on their salvation in Christ. He concludes this argument by saying, "Thus Paul's advice to the Roman Christians to subject themselves to Rome was not offered primarily for prudential reasons (not only to avoid retribution), but also because participation in Israel's cause would defeat a central purpose of the gospel for which Christ died."[37]

Additionally, Borg notes the significance of Paul's lack of discussion regarding the evils of human government in his endorsement of submission.[38] We have already discussed how this can be considered from a literalist's perspective, however, it makes even more sense from a contextual perspective. Again, Borg notes that Paul would have had extensive knowledge of the evils perpetrated by the Jewish and Gentile rulers of old due to

35. Ibid., 205.
36. Ibid., 217.
37. Ibid., 218.
38. Ibid., 217.

his prior studies. Paul would have been familiar with the wickedness of the contemporary Roman government as well. However, Paul's silence on these subjects is only surprising if Paul intended for Romans 13 to be a *universal statement of Christian political philosophy* with the intention of legitimizing human government as a normative good. If read as such, it seems to be sloppy and inconsistent with the rest of what we do see in scripture regarding civil government. It also reads as purely naive. But if read as a specific argument for, as Borg describes, "negotiating a specific political crisis,"[39] Paul's argument is a reasonable and strategically inspired message for the Christians of Rome during that specific time period. Thus, the passage makes sense, especially in the context of the rest of the letter to the Romans.

Even if one thinks that we ought to interpret Paul's reference to authority as an exclusive reference to political authority, Borg's argument for interpreting Romans 13 by its historical and textual context (both in the narrower sense of the rest of the letter to the Romans as well as the larger context of what the Bible says about government), makes a compelling case for why we should reject Romans 13 as a guiding statement of Christian political philosophy. This would mean that Romans 13 is an important exhortation that can, at best, teach the modern Christian about handling the sufferings of this world. However, under Borg's interpretative framework, it cannot be used as a statement of political philosophy to legitimize modern states in any way, nor convey to modern Christians a binding command of obedience to such states.

When we turn to First Peter 2:13–17, we realize some very similar conclusions:

> Be subject for the Lord's sake to every human institution, whether it be to the emperor as supreme, or to governors as sent by him to punish those who do evil and to praise those who do good. For this is the will of God, that by doing good you should put to silence the ignorance of foolish people. Live as people who are free, not using your freedom as a cover-up for evil, but living as servants of God. Honor everyone. Love the brotherhood. Fear God. Honor the emperor.

At first glance, First Peter 2 seems just as challenging to libertarian Christians as Romans 13. First Peter 2 says that we must both fear God and honor the emperor in practically the same breath. It also says to be subject, for the Lord's sake, to every human institution, including the Roman

39. Ibid., 218.

Empire. Not only should Peter's audience be subject to the empire, but they should do it for the Lord's sake. Peter also relies on Paul's rhetoric when he speaks of obeying governors who are sent by the emperor to punish evil and to praise those who do good.

In reality, not only does the same argument from historical context apply here, but an even more compelling argument emerges when we consider the logic of First Peter 2. Obviously, like Paul, Peter most likely wrote to discourage sentiments of political revolution and religious zealotry in the face of a tyrannical government. Like Paul, he sought to bring the focus of the early church back to the gospel of Christ and the power of salvation that it brings, which is far and above any earthly power.

For the sake of argument, let us put aside the historical context and choose to interpret the verse in its most literal sense and with a binding command on all Christians beyond the time period in which Peter wrote, which is decidedly anti-libertarian by all counts. However, this literal and binding interpretation is ultimately a rather absurd position to take by any Christian who wants to both be a Christian and have anything to do with contemporary politics.

To evaluate this contention, consider the transition from the medieval rule by monarchs to the Enlightenment's spread of limited representative governments subject to the people. Peter argued that Christians had an obligation to obey and honor the emperor, the king, and his appointed governors. Taken literally, this should mean that Christians during the Enlightenment ought to have opposed any notions of popular rule—choosing to honor the king. Yet, many Christians participated in and drove the conversation toward representative government. Some of them even helped to topple dictatorial monarchs. As a result, we live in a time where representative political systems that incorporate extensive voting rights are considered the norm in Western governments. But this was not always so—and many Christians helped drive the transition.

However, a truly literal interpretation of First Peter 2 would nullify all contemporary political participation in modern democracies by Christians since such participation is the inheritance of disobedience toward previous political regimes. In fact, any Christian who is inspired by the idea of America but who also would hold that we should interpret First Peter 2 as literal and binding would be wise to check themselves—the United States as it exists today would not have been possible absent the open defiance of the American colonists in the eighteenth century.

While some Christians may be tempted to follow the argument to such conclusions, this ultimately seems untenable. It would imply that being a Christian is only possible so long as one retains a respect for kingly civil authority. This conclusion is as absurd as it sounds, yet it must follow from those who choose to take this passage as absolutely literal and universally binding. It also makes the mistake of connecting the eternal significance of the Christian faith with ultimately temporal political viewpoints.

Some Christians will likely soften this literal perspective, but seek to retain the spirit of the "literal" command by retranslating its meaning for the era of modern democracy. Thus, they might interpret this passage to now mean that Christians ought to honor the president or the prime minister since today's political authority is now democratic. However, in making this interpretative decision, Christians are guilty of proof-texting a verse in order to make it fit within the context of their current political situation (which conveniently ignores all of the disobedience that was necessary to establish their current political situation). Furthermore, they are using the verse to attempt to accomplish something Peter almost certainly never intended to do, which is to formulate a Christian statement of political philosophy with regard to the subject of political legitimacy.

Thus, as with Romans 13, it makes sense to lean in favor of interpreting First Peter 2 as a historically contextual exhortation and not a binding statement of Christian political philosophy. When considering First Peter 2 in this light, we realize that it does not provide sufficient grounds for Christians to reject the libertarian skepticism of political power. It merely provides another example of a recommendation to submit to political authority as a means of deterring the human desire to make political revolution the church's aspiration.

Render unto Caesar

With the concerns over First Peter 2 and Romans 13 addressed, the libertarian Christian must now wrestle with the words of Christ himself, as recorded in the Gospels of Matthew and Luke:

> Then the Pharisees went and plotted how to entangle him in his words. And they sent their disciples to him, along with the Herodians, saying, "Teacher, we know that you are true and teach the way of God truthfully, and you do not care about anyone's opinion, for you are not swayed by appearances. Tell us, then, what you

WHAT DOES THE BIBLE SAY ABOUT GOVERNMENT?

think. Is it lawful to pay taxes to Caesar, or not?" But Jesus, aware of their malice, said, "Why put me to the test, you hypocrites? Show me the coin for the tax." And they brought him a denarius. And Jesus said to them, "Whose likeness and inscription is this?" They said, "Caesar's." Then he said to them, "Therefore render to Caesar the things that are Caesar's, and to God the things that are God's." When they heard it, they marveled. And they left him and went away.[40]

The scribes and the chief priests sought to lay hands on him at that very hour, for they perceived that he had told this parable against them, but they feared the people. So they watched him and sent spies, who pretended to be sincere, that they might catch him in something he said, so as to deliver him up to the authority and jurisdiction of the governor. So they asked him, "Teacher, we know that you speak and teach rightly, and show no partiality, but truly teach the way of God. Is it lawful for us to give tribute to Caesar, or not?" But he perceived their craftiness, and said to them, "Show me a denarius. Whose likeness and inscription does it have?" They said, "Caesar's." He said to them, "Then render to Caesar the things that are Caesar's, and to God the things that are God's." And they were not able in the presence of the people to catch him in what he said, but marveling at his answer they became silent.[41]

In both accounts, we seem to have a command from Jesus Christ himself to "render unto Caesar that which is Caesar's," a seemingly irrefutable command to pay taxes. Perhaps even more so than the first two passages from Paul and Peter, these passages have been quoted from the pulpit and in private conversations as a means of legitimizing both the Christian's obligation to pay taxes and the political authority to issue taxes. How is that possible to reexamine with a libertarian perspective?

If we read the text carefully, noting the context of the answer that Jesus gave, a deeper meaning of the passage beyond the political connotation becomes quickly apparent. The Pharisees asked Jesus about whether or not they should pay taxes to the Roman government. Both Matthew and Luke note that the Pharisees had a specific goal in mind: to entice Jesus into saying something inflammatory, something that would violate Roman law and allow them to turn him over to the Roman authorities. Both Matthew and Luke also note that Jesus sensed their malicious intent in articulating

40. Matt 22:15–22
41. Luke 20:19–26

65

his answer. This is significant because it demonstrates that Jesus was not simply giving a teaching, like the Sermon on the Mount, but that he was playing an intellectual game of chess with the Pharisees. He had to choose his words carefully lest he fall into their trap. And so he did, telling his audience to render unto Caesar that which is Caesar's and unto God that which is God's.

Christians often interpret this command by focusing on the first half of the verse ("Render unto Caesar the things that are Caesar's"), but the mistake they make is to ignore the placement of this statement next to the second half of the saying ("Render unto God the things that are God's"). Let us consider the logic of focusing on this passage as a command to render unto Caesar that which is Caesar's as an independent commandment that is separate from the second half of the saying.

In the first place, it implies that Caesar can lay claim to certain things that God cannot lay claim to. If we are to render unto Caesar that which is Caesar's and to God that which is God's, how do we know where Caesar's claim of authority ends and God's begins? Remember, the two statements about "rendering" in this passage were made to contrast with each other. If the contrasting language means that Caesar can rightfully lay a claim of authority to anything: loyalty, taxes, respect, obedience, etc., then it is done so in contrast with the authority of God. This clearly contradicts basic Christian doctrine about God's authority over all kingdoms and earthly powers. C.S. Lewis rebutted the idea of Caesar having unique claims against God in *The Weight of Glory* when he wrote, "He who surrenders himself without reservation to the temporal claims of a nation, or a party, or a class, is rendering to Caesar that which, of all things, most emphatically belongs to God: himself."[42]

As Christians, we know that there is nothing that Caesar can claim over which God does not have total and absolute authority. We also know that this was a brilliant answer if we focus on the second half of the command, "render unto God that which is God's." We can assume that Jesus, being God, knew that there is *nothing* in this world that Caesar can lay claim to that is not God's. Jesus not only evaded the Pharisees' cross-examination tactics, but he also provided his followers with a powerful dichotomy that should help us focus our attention on the greater authority and power of God than of Caesar.

42. Lewis, *The Weight of Glory*, 53.

Yet, most Christians accept the mainstream view that this passage is about paying taxes and the legitimacy of taxation. This is a boring and timid thesis, at best, and a misunderstanding of the intent of the passage at worst. God is Lord over all creation, and he has the first rights on anything that Caesar might ask for, including our loyalty, obedience, and money. Christians should zoom in on this passage with the goal of seeing how God is above Caesar, recognizing that not even taxes are something that Caesar can rightfully lay claim to in the presence of God. This passage is not about rendering taxes and power to Caesar, but about pointing us back to the highest King above all kings who makes all Caesars weak and puny before him.

Thus, after surveying a number of passages in scripture that discuss government, the claim that scripture invalidates libertarianism makes little sense. Especially when the Big Four are combined with the passages I highlighted earlier, a biblical case emerges for holding the claims of legitimacy by earthly political authorities skeptically, choosing to view God as the highest of all authorities, and focusing first and foremost on the protection of the innocent in matters of social importance. All of these notions are compatible with the libertarian desire to minimize the abuses of state power and maximize individual rights.

CALVIN RESPONDS

It is essential to observe that these interpretations of the "Big Four" have their detractors. Theologian John Calvin represents perhaps the most ardent opponent. Calvin zealously argued for obedience to political authorities in his *Institutes of the Christian Religion* as a deeply biblical principle. He relied heavily on Romans 13 and First Peter 2 to justify his argument in saying that, "The first duty of subjects toward their rulers, is to entertain the most honorable views of the office, recognizing it as a delegated jurisdiction from God, and on that account receiving and reverencing them as the ministers and ambassadors of God."[43]

Calvin took a hyperliteral reading of these texts and carried it to its logical conclusion—all Christian believers have a binding duty to honor and submit to human political authorities out of the utmost reverence. It should be noted that many contemporary Christians might accept Calvin's adherence to literally interpreting these passages while rejecting the logical conclusion of near total submission. However, even in this position, many

43. John Calvin, *Institutes of the Christian Religion*, 983.

Christians still accept that these passages do carry a binding meaning about the importance of honoring and obeying political authorities from a biblical perspective—meaning that First Peter and Romans 13 teach, beyond their specific cultural context, that Christians ought to obey and submit to earthly governments as a general principle.

Many Christians who are less extreme than Calvin will tease out various nuances for the principle of submission. The goal in doing so is to account for instances of political disobedience in the Old Testament or to reconcile Christian participation in the American revolution or in assassination efforts against a tyrant like Hitler by men like Dietrich Bonhoeffer.[44] Maybe disobedience is justified in the case of extreme evil by political authority. Maybe disobedience is justified when a duly appointed body of elected representatives are at its forefront. Maybe disobedience is justified after "a long train of abuses." This list of possible exceptions goes on, and many Christians agree to some of them.

Ultimately, however, most Christians accept the notion of political authority as legitimate and worthy of obedience in most cases, with exceptions such as those above teased out. The rule is obedience; the exception is disobedience. Thus, any Christians who accept these passages as both literal and binding with regard to the concept of legitimizing political authority are *on some point along Calvin's scale of advocating for political authority.* Some of these Christians disagree with Calvin regarding the level of obligation that they have to earthly regimes to a greater degree than others.

Ironically, I consider myself a Calvinist, and I think Calvin was dead wrong on this issue. Calvin made some significant errors when he turned to his discussion of civil authority in the *Institutes* for the following reasons:

1. Scripture must interpret scripture. There are many other passages in scripture that might give us valid reason to reexamine Calvin's interpretation of Romans 13 and First Peter 2 as statements of Christian political philosophy. The themes of those passages have already been addressed in this chapter.

---

44. It should be noted that Calvin, along with many other Christians, does concede that the Christian is allowed to disobey political authority when political authority requires the Christian to disobey God. Calvin makes this exception explicit in the *Institutes*, arguing: "But in that obedience which we hold to be due to the commands of rulers, must always make the exception, no, must be particularly careful that it is not incompatible with obedience to Him to whose will the wishes of all kings should be subject, to whose decrees their commands must yield to whose majesty their scepters must bow" (Calvin, *Institutes of the Christian Religion*, 988).

2. Christians should not solely use scripture to authoritatively speak into political philosophy, especially without a thorough background in the topic they are addressing. Calvin makes this mistake, although one cannot fault him entirely as many outstanding libertarian arguments have been made in the past two hundred years—well after his death. However, many Christians use Calvin's reasoning or otherwise literally accept First Peter 2 and Romans 13 as binding commands that demand political obedience and establish legitimate political authority. They believe this in spite of good arguments from libertarians about why disobeying certain laws or political regimes is a good thing. Similarly, if a libertarian argues that the state is illegitimate or at best, a necessary evil, Christians typically reject such a claim on its face. If a libertarian is advancing an otherwise logically coherent argument for why political authority is dangerous or why it should be delegitimized, Christians have an obligation to listen to the argument and respond to it by assessing the argument on its merits. Otherwise, they engage in proof-texting and rely upon scripture to justify political opinions, which otherwise may not stand up in the face of opposing arguments.

3. In advancing a scriptural interpretation of political authority, Christians must not also advance a position that ethically contradicts itself. The notion that all (or most) political authority is God-given and thus, ought to be obeyed can easily become a violation of basic Christian ethical commitments. For instance, if the Bible tells us that we should not murder, Christians should not pay for policies that murder innocent people, such as a drone strike program or abortion subsidies. Yet in advocating obedience to political authority (whether nearly unlimited, as Calvin argued for, or some other modified general principle of submission), Christians put themselves in the position of honoring and paying for policies that murder innocent people. This should trouble Christians deeply.

Following up on the last point, even if one accepts Calvin's exception to disobey rulers when they command one to disobey God (or even other exceptions), the logical conflict that emerges between Christian ethics and political obligation precludes any possibility of piecing together a coherent political framework. What does it mean to disobey God by disobeying political rulers? Would it be disobedient to God to pay taxes to a government when one knows those taxes are supporting a government that funds abortions, initiates foreign wars that lead to hundreds of thousands of dead civilians (some of whom are fellow Christians), funds terrorist groups, and drives honest entrepreneurs out of business through excessive fines and regulations?

Some Christians might respond that, obviously, we pay those taxes given that nothing our government does today could be as bad as what the dictators of the ancient world did when Paul and Peter wrote. If they thought it was important to obey such an oppressive government, how could we, as Christians living in modern day America, find reason to delegitimize the authority of the US government?

This position seems tenuous at best. King David watched Bathsheba bathe naked and then had her husband killed so he could add her to his harem of wives. He was also called a man after God's own heart. Yet we do not take David's example to mean that modern Christian men should watch other men's wives bathing and then murder their husbands. We ought to also remember that King David was a polygamist who had many wives. Yet, this fact does not mean that modern Christian men should have several wives. Likewise, Paul and Peter saw fit to encourage the early Christian church to obey an overtly tyrannical government for specific reasons in a given political climate. This fact does not mean that we ought to accept tyrannical governments as moral in our political philosophy, especially when better political philosophies exist now than were in existence during the period of the early church.

Thus, it is unconvincing to use Romans 13, First Peter 2, Matthew 22, and Luke 20 as justifications for political authority or to reject libertarianism. Even assuming, for the sake of argument, that all political authority is from God, it does not follow from this idea that all societies must *normatively* exist under a state with an exclusive monopoly on the use of legitimate violence and the power to tax. If ordered and working societies emerged without a centralized state for governance, it would certainly be possible to remain a Christian in such a society—in the same way that it has remained possible to be a Christian in an age of democracy compared to an age of monarchy.

TOWARD A MORE AUGUSTINIAN VIEW OF GOVERNMENT

With a new understanding of Romans 13, First Peter 2, and the phrase, "Render unto Caesar," we must consider: what next? It is important to note

70

that we must not feel obligated to adopt a political philosophy out of a desire to find the one and only "Christian political philosophy." Libertarianism is not Christianity, progressivism is not Christianity, and conservatism is not Christianity. But, practically speaking, why is libertarianism a better political philosophy for Christians?

For one, libertarianism allows for Christians to, in the context of political discussions, rightfully focus issues on the injustices perpetrated against individuals by state power. In fact, many secular libertarians are far more effective in seeing people as people when political issues are raised than those Christians who choose to side with government authorities in enforcing the law and expanding the scope of its interventions.

For instance, Christians should consider immigration policy in light of the fact that immigrants—both legal and illegal—are human beings created in the image of God. Many immigrants come to America to make a living for themselves and their families. Some of them are Christians. Current immigration restrictions harm these people, giving them no alternative but to enter the country illegally if they want the opportunity to pursue a better life. Yet, many Christians support these restrictions while many libertarians oppose these restrictions.

Libertarianism also pulls the blinders off of Christians who fail to see the reality of sin in the context of political power. On some issues, the church has done a fantastic job of beating the drum of national loyalty and law and order without leaving room for nuance regarding many of the harsh realities of government policies—harsh realities that result from sinful people making and enforcing laws.

As an illustration, thousands of good, innocent people have been killed by American bombings and drone strikes in foreign interventions in the Middle East. Some of these people were Christians. Yet, many American Christians support foreign wars and interventions in the name of fighting the War on Terror, often ignoring the dramatic cost in innocent human life. The libertarian argument against our hawkish foreign policy (though many libertarians support military action in self-defense) emphasizes opening up trade routes and peacefully exchanging goods and services with individuals in other nations. Rather than spreading democracy abroad through violence and military might, libertarians encourage a foreign policy that maximizes and respects the freedom of individuals rather than the might of a particular nation-state.

For decades, libertarians have been decrying the overly harsh response to drugs as manifested in drug war policies. Thousands upon thousands of purely nonviolent drug users have been locked in cages, subject to violent arrests, or even had friends and family harmed by law enforcement officials either for using or being suspected of using drugs. Yet, many Christians support the overly harsh War on Drugs.

Instead of following the arguments of John Calvin or otherwise accepting a modified literalist interpretation of passages like Romans 13, Christians can do better in speaking truth, justice, and mercy in the political arena. A great place to start for developing a robustly Christian perspective of government that is compatible with libertarianism is to go back in the lineage of Christian theology to the early fifth century. St. Augustine's magnum opus, *City of God*, should be required reading for any Christian who wants to seriously grapple with their views on the role of government while maintaining a deeply theological joy in the gospel and superiority of Christ.

Central to Augustine's thesis in *City of God* was his claim that God had divided humankind into two cities—the city of God, which is the "heavenly city," and the city of man, which is the "earthly city." Robert Kraynak defined Augustine's concept of the heavenly city as, "the spiritual association of all those who love God more than the world."[45] Augustine believed that these believers, predestined by God to glory in the life to come, walk through this earth as pilgrims, finding contentment and enjoyment in the present journey while ever looking forward to the marvels at its end. Meanwhile, the unregenerate in the city of man infatuate themselves with the love of self and earthly things, choosing to focus on the good life in the present without adequate care for the things eternal. Augustine wrote that,

> Two cities have been formed by two loves: the earthly by the love of self, even to the contempt of God; the heavenly by the love of God, even to the contempt of self. The former, in a word, glories in itself, the latter in the Lord. For the one seeks glory from men; but the greatest glory of the other is God, the witness of conscience.[46]

The city of man, according to Augustine, was defined by its thirst for power and self-glorification. On this basis, Augustine frequently launched himself into scathing criticisms of both Roman political authority and more generally, the concept of political authority. At one point in the *City*

45. Kraynak, *Christian Faith and Modern Democracy*, 90.
46. Augustine, *City of God*, 477.

of God, after proving that the achievement of true justice was an impossible dream in a society of sinful men, Augustine said the following:

> Justice being taken away, then, what are kingdoms but great robberies? For what are robberies themselves, but little kingdoms? The band itself is made up of men; it is ruled by the authority of a prince, it is knit together by a pact of the confederacy; the booty is divided by the law agreed on. If, by the admittance of abandoned men this evil increases to such a degree that it holds places, fixes abodes, takes possession of cities, and subdues peoples, it assumes the more plainly the name of a kingdom.[47]

Here, Augustine identified both of the key characteristics of the state. He realized that the state, like bands of thieves, collects its revenue by compelling individuals to pay tribute (*compulsory taxation*). He also realized that eventually, the state would govern in a specific region (*territorial monopoly*). Furthermore, not being content to merely compare kingdoms to robber bands, Augustine, in the same selection, proceeded to illustrate his disgust with the coercive robber function of the state by recounting the story of a pirate. Captured by Alexander the Great, the captain of a pirate ship was brought to the emperor for an audience. After Alexander had asked the pirate what he meant by taking "hostile possession of the sea," Augustine recorded that the pirate gave an "apt and true reply" saying, "What thou meanest by seizing the whole earth; but because I do it with a petty ship, I am called a robber, whilst thou who dost it with a great fleet art styled emperor."[48]

Augustine did not stop at comparing kingdoms to robber bands and empires to pirate fleets. He later compared the method by which political leaders rule to the method by which demons deceive:

> For just as the demons cannot possess any but those whom they have deceived with guile, so also men in princely office, not indeed being just, but like demons, have persuaded the people in the name of religion to receive as true those things which they themselves knew to be false; in this way, as it were, binding them up more firmly in civil society, so that they might in like manner possess them as subjects. But who that was weak and unlearned

---

47. Ibid., 112.
48. Ibid., 113.

could escape the deceits of both the princes of the state and the demons?[49]

Thus, it is hard to imagine a Christian with a lower perspective of human political authority than St. Augustine. One cannot rightfully call him a libertarian, especially in the modern sense of the term, but his criticisms of state power prove consistent with the history of governments and the biblical themes outlined in this chapter. They also are happily at home amid the criticisms of the state launched by libertarians.

However, Augustine did not merely criticize political authority and throw up his hands in despair at their wickedness. Augustine saw the answer to political authority not in violent revolution or aspiration to power as a counterbalance but instead promoted the Christian ideals of charity and grace. Augustine knew that the city of man is not the permanent city of the believer but only a temporary dwelling place. He also knew that evil could not be combatted with evil. In Augustine's view, Christians should not aspire to power, but pursue first and foremost, the things of God, allowing them to be our source of hope and joy.

> But the reward of the saints is far different, who even here endured reproaches for that city of God which is hateful to the lovers of this world. That city is eternal. There none are born, for none die. There is true and fully felicity—not a goddess, but a gift of God. Thence we receive the pledge of faith, whilst on our pilgrimage we sight for its beauty. There rises not the sun on the good and the evil, but the Sun of Righteousness protects the good alone. There no great industry shall be expended to enrich the public treasury by suffering privations at home, for there is the common treasury of truth.[50]

WHAT NOW?

So where does this leave us: are Christians biblically obligated to support the idea that governmental authority is inherently legitimate or to argue for the expansion of its powers, contra libertarianism? It is difficult to answer in the affirmative. Christians can agree with the following three statements without contradicting the core doctrines of our faith:

---

49. Ibid., 140.
50. Ibid., 166.

1. Christ is my savior and is Lord and King over all creation. I have been redeemed through his sacrifice at the cross and forgiven of my sins. He rose from the dead and is seated at the right hand of God the Father. The knowledge of this wonderful reality has been communicated through the infallible, revealed text of scripture.

2. Humans are depraved, corrupted by sin, and deal with the struggles and evils associated with that sin every day. This holds true for all individuals, whether they work in government or not.

3. Society is far better off with a much more limited government that only serves a few limited functions or no government at all.

To hold that the third statement somehow invalidates or is inconsistent with the first two statements makes no sense. Moreover, scripture provides Christians with enough ammunition to be rationally skeptical about the political process, given the realities of human sin. As long as this skepticism is grounded in good theology and a commitment to realism, libertarianism is not an unhealthy or contradictory position for the Christian to embrace.

WHY LIBERTARIANISM?

According to a libertarian view, actions that physically harm innocent individuals without their consent are almost always unjustified. Violating the principle of nonaggression is a grave misstep because it allows for a host of other violations of the rights and dignity of individual human beings. When does the slippery slope of injustice stop? And again, why trust human political authorities with the power to make these decisions in the first place?

Thus, the libertarian emphasis, while not a total worldview, provides a powerful political ethic for the committed Christian. It helps Christians understand and realize the dangers of political power and seek to mitigate those dangers out of a desire to protect the innocent. It gives us an ethical framework for recognizing how we can work toward a world where the powerful are held in check and the oppressed are comforted.

This is the part where I get a bit personal. As stated at the outset of this chapter, I do not believe that the state can be an ethically legitimate entity. I personally long for a society where the state does not exist—this makes me an anarcho-capitalist. More importantly than simply longing for such a society, I truly believe that it can happen in a modern country. The realization of a free society without a centralized state does not require the wholesale abolition of all governments, Molotov cocktails, Guy Fawkes masks, or looting gangs. It only requires that individuals be allowed to opt out of current nation-based systems of government and to peacefully establish new governance structures that require consent and rely on competition to produce the best outcomes. Promising new technologies may give us the potential to accomplish these ends in the coming decades.

In the past six years, a new currency has emerged and is quickly gaining ground. Known as Bitcoin, it relies on a peer-to-peer network of miners to process and confirm transactions that are made using the currency. To confirm that the transactions are accurately processed, all Bitcoin transactions are recorded on a public ledger known as the blockchain. If you do not understand this technical explanation of Bitcoin at the moment, that is perfectly fine. The key point is that Bitcoin, from its inception to today, has operated entirely as a decentralized currency, outside of the control of any central bank or regulating body. The blockchain is a decentralized technological breakthrough that might end up changing our lives in ways far beyond the scope of Bitcoin. Entrepreneurs, coders, and cryptographers are already exploring ways to use the concept of the blockchain to serve as a decentralized solution for organizational structures, contracts, and investment. As a result of the peer-to-peer nature of the networks associated with this technology, there's no central source of regulation or control—and especially no way to use violence to coerce everyone in the network to behave in a specified way. Bitcoin, and the potential to use the blockchain, could produce the same sort of freeing effect on finances, contracts, legal institutions, and business structures that the Internet did for free speech.

Likewise, 3D printing technology has the potential to highly decentralize product manufacturing using cost effective methods. The technology works by allowing users to input designs for a product into a 3D printing machine—the machine uses various materials to build the object for the user on the spot. If it becomes widely used, 3D printing may allow individuals to produce any variety of products in their own home, free from the prying eyes of regulatory agencies.

As a Christian, I am ready to participate in and embrace these improvements, regardless of whether or not a state is involved or at the helm. I do not need a state in my political philosophy in order to follow my savior, and I do not need a state in my political philosophy in order to realize the potential that exists in front of us to make the world a better place with new ideas and innovative solutions.

In addition, Christians should be open to libertarianism for another important reason: being on the right side of a moral debate in the long run. Michael Huemer, a contemporary philosopher, argues that in the next several hundred years, it might be possible to see a widespread disavowal of the notion of political authority in the same way that we today disavow slavery, even though slavery was ethically acceptable for thousands of years.[51] To justify his argument, Huemer argues that political authority has an inherent flaw that makes the whole concept morally dysfunctional. He points out that, "Acts that would be considered unjust or morally unacceptable when performed by nongovernmental agents will often be considered perfectly all right, even praiseworthy, when performed by government agents . . . Why do we accord this special moral status to government and are we justified in so doing? This is the problem of political authority."[52]

Huemer is completely right in pointing out this conundrum. Governments have done many things that we consider to be good simply because we deem the government to wield legitimate political authority—yet these same actions would strike us as deeply immoral if we observed private citizens engaging in the same behavior. Even if we do agree that many government actions are morally wrong, we still often accept political legitimacy as a sufficient excuse for allowing said immoral behavior.

When any government collects taxes, it essentially issues a threat to all of its subjects—we have already discussed this in a descriptive fashion earlier, but now it is time to be a bit more normative. The threat is that, if subjects fail to pay, they will be jailed for a lengthy period of time. Men with guns will enforce this mandate if necessary. Now, imagine if any private individual or company issued the same threat—we would immediately regard such action as immoral.

When government enforces laws against nonviolent crimes, such as the prohibition of certain drugs, it issues a threat against individuals who decide to use those drugs. Men with guns will also enforce those laws and take people to jail who refuse to obey, even if those people have not harmed anyone in the process of buying, selling, or consuming those drugs. Here's the rub: if private citizens started breaking into each other's homes to ensure that their neighbors were not using drugs with which we morally disagreed, everyone would see the immoral and illegitimate nature of such behavior.

51. Huemer, *The Problem of Political Authority*, 332–33.

52. Ibid., 4–5.

Why do badges and uniforms grant any special authority to engage in the same behavior?

If the government decides that it ought to take naked pictures of airline passengers, rifle through our suitcases, and rough up children and the elderly, we allow it. It's called the Transportation Security Agency. Of course, if private individuals engaged in this behavior on a routine basis, we would not stand for it. We would opt for other alternatives to ensure our security that do not require the potential levels of humiliation inherent in current TSA practices.

These are small examples that illustrate Huemer's point: government operates under a different set of moral rules and consequently engages in immoral behaviors with a perceived sense of legitimacy. Carried to logical conclusions, as government powers expand, the scope and abuse of these behaviors increases as more individuals suffer from the injustices of the state's initiation of aggressive violence. Huemer sees no basis for legitimizing this violence and abuse when we apply the same moral rules to government actions as we do to private actions. If you are interested in exploring this topic further, consider reading Huemer's arguments in *The Problem of Political Authority*.

Someday, moral sentiments may change and people may start to recognize the moral absurdity of the very concept of political authority. I am optimistic that more and more individuals will recognize that Huemer is right: that state power is as startlingly illegitimate as previous moral evils that were culturally acceptable for thousands of years.

If this revolution in moral sentiments comes about with regard to political legitimacy, Christians must be at the forefront. Throughout history, many Christians have taken the wrong moral positions on societal issues—sometimes even on the grounds that the Bible supported their position. Some Christians used to argue that slavery and capital punishment for homosexual behavior were morally good things because they could be found in the Bible. The history of Christianity in Europe is a history of religious warfare and persecution between different sects and denominations. Religious disagreements between different denominations became grounds for torture and death.

Whether simply misguided or downright Christian in name only, many Christians (and alleged Christians) have unfortunately been guilty of defending pretty stupid things over the course of history. It may be a few hundred years from now, but political authority may be on the horizon. Do we want to leave a legacy for future generations that Christianity teaches that immoral behaviors are acceptable when government actors engage in them—and that we must perpetuate the legitimacy of supporting those wrongdoings by obeying, honoring, and paying tribute to such governments? Personally, this is not an intellectual or moral legacy I wish to leave behind.

Better than accepting contemporary evils in the status quo is when Christians stand up against them—and many Christians have done so. Standing in defense of their fellow man, there were other Christians who helped runaway slaves along their journey to Canada, who sought to abolish slavery altogether, and who called for peace in the midst of religious warfare. In doing so, they defended the dignity of their fellow man, regardless of religious or social status and demanded that justice be equally applied to all. These are the Christians we need to emulate when we consider political authority and the consequences of legitimizing an entire institution on the basis of aggressive violence against its subjects.

Thus, on the issue of political authority, contemporary advances in political thought through libertarianism give us, as Christians, the opportunity to be at the forefront of a very important moral debate. In doing so, I think Christians have the opportunity to realize why Augustine called kingdoms nothing more than "grand robberies" while pointing back to the Christian values of charity and grace as an alternative to political domination.

Frederic Bastiat concluded *The Law* by encouraging his readers to do away with systems and "to try liberty . . . which is an act of faith in God and His work."[53] I can hardly do better than Bastiat. As Christians, we should join Bastiat in rejecting those systems that harm individuals and that attempt to water down the gospel of Christ into a political party. We should cease idolizing the state by viewing it as a fountain of law and morality and instead recognize it for what it really is—a bunch of sinners who often think too much of themselves. We should put aside pretentious notions of the sacred halls of government and, as Augustine said, choose to see things as they plainly are, regardless of the alleged greatness and glory of political rulers. We should realize that the answer to human sinfulness is not to concentrate power in the hands of sinful humans but to decentralize power.

In short, as Christians, we should agree with Bastiat and try liberty for a change and leave our desire to control, mold, and fix others up to God's sovereignty. Only he can change men's hearts, only he can fix sinners, and only he is worthy of honor, reverence, and unlimited obedience.

53. Bastiat, *The Law*, 55.

BIBLIOGRAPHY

Augustine. The City of God. Translated by Marcus Dods. New York: Modern Library, 1993.

Bastiat, Frederic. The Law. Auburn: Ludwig von Mises Institute, 2007.

Block, Walter. "Libertarianism vs. Libertinism." The Journal of Libertarian Studies 11 (1994): 117–128. https://mises.org/library/libertarianism-and-libertinism.

Borg, Marcus. "A New Context for Romans XIII." New Testament Studies 19 (1973): 205–218.

Calvin, John. Institutes of the Christian Religion. Peabody, MA: Hendrickson, 2008.

Carter, Stephen. "Law Puts Us All in the Same Danger as Eric Garner." Bloomberg View, December 4, 2014. https://www.bloomberg.com/view/articles/2014–12-04/law-puts-us-all-in-same-danger-as-eric-garner.

Graham, Franklin. "Franklin Graham's Facebook page." Facebook, March 12, 2015. https://www.facebook.com/FranklinGraham/posts/883361438386705.

The Guardian, "'I Can't Breathe': Eric Garner Put in Chokehold by NYPD Officer—Video," December 4, 2014, video file, http://www.theguardian.com/us-news/video/2014/dec/04/i-cant-breathe-eric-garner-chokehold-death-video.

Hoppe, Hans-Hermann. Democracy: The God That Failed. New Brunswick: Transaction, 2001.

Huemer, Michael. The Problem of Political Authority. New York: Palgrave Macmillan, 2013.

Kraynak, Robert. Christian Faith and Modern Democracy. Notre Dame: University of Notre Dame Press, 2001.

Lewis, C.S. The Weight of Glory. New York: Harper Collins, 1980.

Paul, Ron. Transcript of Farewell Address. November 14, 2014. http://www.campaignforliberty.org/national-blog/transcript-of-farewell-address/.

Rummel, RJ. 20th Century Democide, November, 23, 2002. https://www.hawaii.edu/powerkills/20TH.HTM.

———. Power Kills. New Brunswick: Transaction, 1997.

Strong, James. Strong's Exhaustive Concordance of the Bible. Peabody, MA: Hendrickson, 2007.

Weber, Max. "Politics as a Vocation." In From Max Weber: Essays in Sociology, edited by H.H. Gerth and C. Wright Mills, 77–128. New York: Oxford University Press, 1946.

3

Cool It: You Don't Have to Be a Libertine

Taylor Barkley

If you are reading this book, you are probably looking for answers on how to apply your personal morals to the political sphere. You have also likely considered libertarianism because libertarians make a compelling case on economic policies—but what about personal morality? Doesn't being a libertarian mean you can't have traditional moral beliefs about sexuality, drugs, and human dignity? That you must not only accept what you might believe to be immoral behavior but also endorse it? If that's the case, then you can't be both a Christian and a libertarian because an amoral lifestyle is not consistent with the Christian lifestyle.[1] However, that is *not* the case. Walter Block, a prominent libertarian economist, wrote, "There is perhaps no greater confusion in all of political economy than that between libertarianism and libertinism. That they are commonly taken for one another is an understatement of the highest order."[2] All of the authors of this book recognize this tension or once had this misconception. But in fact, the opposite is true: you can keep your view of personal morality. You don't have to be a libertine to be a libertarian.

Many conservatives are aware of libertarianism, but the perceived implications of libertarian political theory on their personal moral framework may be one of the reasons, or even the main reason, they consider

1. "If you love me, you will keep my commandments" (John 14:15).
2. Block, "Libertarianism and Libertinism," 117.

themselves conservative instead of libertarian. Because this concern cuts two ways, there may be those of the opposite persuasion: their libertarian beliefs may prevent them from becoming a Christian or even from merely respecting Christian beliefs. But one can remain entirely orthodox in Christian moral beliefs and be a libertarian. Furthermore, there are ways Christians can communicate their moral beliefs in a loving, effective manner that does not match up with the common misperception of social conservatives. Libertarian does not necessarily mean libertine. For me, this was a very real philosophical conflict that I was determined to reconcile.

Before going further, we need to define these two terms. In chapter 2, Jason Hughey defines libertarianism "simply as a political philosophy that is 'concerned solely with the proper use of force. Its core premise is that it should be illegal to threaten or initiate violence against a person or his property without his permission; force is justified only in defense or retaliation.'" That is the definition used in this chapter. "Libertine" refers to "a person who is unrestrained by convention or morality; one leading a dissolute life."[3] In this chapter, the term will also imply a moral relativism—a "what is right for you may be wrong for me" attitude—and that morality is outside the realm of objective truth.

MY OWN STORY

In junior high and high school, when I participated in a homeschooling co-op, I was taught a strict, consistently Christian worldview of one-to-one correspondence between biblical moral teachings and how I should live my life. This is part of what it meant to "live in a Christian manner."

In high school, I was assigned to read Thomas Sowell's *Basic Economics*. Sowell's free-market economics were so counterintuitive, so surprising, and so reasonable that the ideas have stuck with me ever since. For example, I distinctly remember supporting a minimum wage when I was in high school, for obvious reasons: I wanted to make more money and believed that other low wage earners deserved the same. But Sowell's free-market arguments against the minimum wage surprised me because they made total sense.

I felt intellectually challenged; like I was opening up a whole new world of knowledge and real-world implications. I saw that free markets

3. *Merriam-Webster Online*, s.v. "libertine." http://www.merriam-webster.com/dictionary/libertine.

and liberty allow human beings to flourish. Government in limited and measured amounts protects the market processes that allocate nearly all the goods and services we need and desire. Economics continues to be one of the primary lenses through which I view public policy. It's also helpful in my personal life, such as when I'm choosing which car to buy.

Later I majored in history and political science at Taylor University—a small, generally conservative Christian college. During a political science class on various political ideologies, my professor said that Christians cannot be libertarians. At the time, I took his word for it. From what I remember of his lecture, he equated "libertarian" to Objectivism. (For a definition and more discussion about Objectivism from a Christian perspective, see Leah's definition in chapter 4). He objected to what he perceived as libertarianism's central belief, that selfishness is a virtue. I now know that's an Objectivist belief but not necessarily a libertarian one. Objectivists can be libertarian, but not all libertarians are Objectivists. My professor was correct that a Christian can't be an Objectivist because of two contradicting beliefs: Christians believe in a God, and strict Objectivists do not. He taught a tight connection between Christian morality and political ideology. At the time, I thought my political philosophy certainly could not trump my Christian theology, so I wrote off the possibility of being a libertarian and thought Christian friends who said they were libertarians were misguided. During and just after my college years, I identified as a conservative.

Like many evangelicals of my generation, I grew disillusioned by the Christian right, which taught a simple worldview of Christian morality defined by "good behavior" with a myopic focus on social platforms in politics, such as campaigns to keep statues of the Ten Commandments on courthouse and statehouse lawns or to educate policymakers and voters about America's Christian heritage. The conservative Christian right seemed to overlook economic and societal well-being. It also seemed to be ineffective and uninspiring for people who weren't social conservatives.

In further evaluating the politics of the Christian right, I also realized that state arbitration of morality and enforcement of moral principles (as preferred by one particular group of people) never seems to produce the desired outcome of a better life for everyone. Even if such moral policing accomplishes this goal for a period of time, when power is inherited by those who don't share the same convictions, oppression can too easily follow. Legal provisions to allow what might indeed be sound moral practices could leave room for truly immoral activity by an abusive state. Why even set the precedent for the abuse of power?

The belief that one's personal Christian morality should completely permeate one's politics is not an uncommon belief. A number of Christian theologians and philosophers have written on this topic. The prominent Christian author and philosopher Dr. Norman Geisler and his coauthor Frank Turek wrote the book *Legislating Morality*, which won the Evangelical Christian Publishers Association Gold Medallion Book Award in 1999. Although the authors do not advocate for legally codifying all of biblical moral law, they do seek to "debunk the myth that 'morality can't be legislated.'"[4] "Christians shouldn't try to set up a Christian government," they say, "but they should try to promote a Christianlike morality (i.e. the Moral Law) in government."[5] They conclude that "America will not stand for extreme Puritanism, nor will it survive radical Libertarianism."[6]

Christian thinker and Houston Baptist University professor, Nancy Pearcey wrote in her book *Total Truth*, "At the core, humans are moral beings, and we long to see our highest moral ideals expressed in our corporate life. Ultimately the secular version of civic life fails to satisfy the human longing to live together in moral communities, committed to Justice and Righteousness."[7] For Pearcey, the secularization of politics and separation from legislated Christian morality brings with it a separation from God's design for human flourishing. I do not disagree with all of Pearcey's writings, merely the political implications. Pearcey, and scholars like Francis Schaeffer before her, have done tremendous work in bringing evangelical theology back to earth, helping evangelicals like me to reconnect theology with my work, my passions, and my interests.

When Southern Baptist Theological Seminary President, Albert Mohler debated Norman Horn, founder and president of Libertarian Christian Institute and author of the foreword in this book, on whether or not Christians can be libertarians,[8] Mohler asserted, "Libertarianism has an extremely difficult time . . . explaining how there could be any right to legal restraints on human liberty in terms of moral behavior."[9]

4. Geisler and Turek, *Legislating Morality*, back cover.
5. Ibid., 104.
6. Ibid., 211.
7. Pearcey, *Total Truth*, 384.
8. Roys, "Can a Christian Be Libertarian?"
9. Ibid.

According to these authors and others, a distinctly Christian perspective on personal morality then *must* have an impact on one's public life. However, this battle to end dualistic thinking was interpreted by me and perhaps others to mean that there should be no separation of thought, that all my moral beliefs—including those about personal morality—should then bleed into my votes and my political activism. For some, this may be the ideal situation, but I don't think it has worked out well throughout history. The "Moral Majority" is now a minority. Both the War on Drugs and Prohibition in the early twentieth century show that the track record ain't good.

Libertarianism as a political philosophy allows for a world in which social conservatives can spend their days on the street corner advocating their moral stance against violent video games or same-sex marriage. But it does not guarantee those beliefs become law. If conservative Christians are speaking out against immorality, they have a right to do so. Libertarianism protects the rights of the 49 percent when the 51 percent want to take them away.

My views are always being refined, but today I hold what would be considered some socially conservative personal moral views and some socially liberal views. But I identify as a libertarian. I believe these views are accurate pictures of how the world works and how we should live in it. God has called us to freedom, not to give in to immoral things but to follow him and to love each other.[10] With personal morality on one hand and a politics centered on liberty on the other, humans are capable of leading flourishing lives as God intended. The Christian objections to libertarianism are based on a correct understanding of Christian morality but often a misunderstanding of libertarianism or a focus on one particular kind of libertarianism. Libertarians do not have to be libertines.

CHRISTIAN MORALITY

In order to unpack this tension between libertarianism and libertinism, it is important to briefly unpack what is meant by Christian morality. Christian morality is found in what God has revealed throughout the Bible and insights from the Holy Spirit. Scripture offers guidance into how God has intended for humans to live.

10. Gal 5.

Christianity is an entirely unique worldview. A religion, by its nature, calls humanity to a higher good and a better way of life: follow these guidelines and you will be redeemed, find joy, and live the good life. But fundamentally, Christian belief is about a relationship, not rules. Christianity makes the bold claim that rules are not central; rather, at its core is the person of Jesus. Jesus is the answer to all the war, suffering, injustice, and sorrow in this world. He came to take our sins and the sins of the world upon himself at no cost to us. Such a sacrifice will and should elicit a response of devotion and fealty to what Christ asks us to do. Humans cannot enter into the kingdom of God on their own accord. We are woefully inadequate and out of our league when it comes to being good moral agents and good in the eyes of God.[11]

This worldview brings a stunning attitude of humility. The knowledge of our sinfulness should make us less judgmental of others. When we have the experience of humility from our own sins, calling another's actions wrong comes from a wholly different posture, for the basic tenets of Christianity mean that I am a sinner too. And if I'm a sinner too, I have a much better understanding of those committing immoral actions.[12]

But because of the Bible, Christians believe they have an objective moral guidebook, a "set of instructions" for how life should be lived and lived well. But remember, these rules aren't the main point of the Bible. The moral and legal guidelines, or the Law, which is outlined in the Hebrew scriptures (the Old Testament), were meant to bring us into closer relationship with God and to show our own shortcomings so that God's grace could be fully exemplified.

The Bible is the record of God's pursuit of humanity as a whole and of humans as individuals. A relationship with God starts with our response to his pursuit. Christians should indeed stand up for their moral convictions, but ultimately that's not what Christianity is about. Because of the many nay-saying voices from Christians themselves, it can be easy to think that Christians condemn things more than they affirm them. Yet Christian beliefs have compelled millions, if not billions, of people to aid their neighbors near and far. Christians have opened hospitals, established schools, conducted disaster relief, started businesses, and more *because* they are Christians.

11. Rom 8
12. Rom 5:20

In light of this emphasis on a relationship with Jesus over moral behavior, why do some Christians insist on legal mandates for their religious beliefs? In one sense, it is consistent for a Christian's faith to take priority over political ideology. Christians believe there is an all-knowing being who has laid out a set of guidelines for how to live well, so it makes sense to follow God's clear dictates over our own thinking on the matter, if those dictates can be understood. A command from an omniscient being is likely worth following, or at least acknowledging, and what is true of God in the personal sphere would naturally then be true of God in the political sphere.

THICK LIBERTARIAN MORALITY
AND THE CHRISTIAN RESPONSE

Oddly enough, many secular libertarians hold the same belief that one can't be a libertarian and a Christian because Christians believe in a specific set of moral standards that would prove "coercive" to others living in opposition to Christian morals.[13] This is the notion of "thick libertarianism," which means that any type of reprimand or judgment is too close to coercion and therefore unlibertarian. Take, for instance, premarital sex. Making a judgment that premarital sex is wrong would be deemed coercive by those having premarital sex, which is unlibertarian; therefore, you can't be a libertarian Christian according to thick libertarianism. They simply don't go together. But are normative moral judgments—saying something *ought* to be such and such a way—coercive? In other words, can I call what my friend is doing or proclaiming "wrong" and still be a libertarian Christian? If normative judgments are coercive, then they would violate the nonaggression principle, thus failing the rubric of many libertarians.

The nonaggression principle, as Jason mentions in chapter 2, is defined in differently nuanced ways, but the common definition seems to come from the Victorian English philosopher Herbert Spencer: "Every man is free to do that which he wills, provided he infringes not the equal freedom of any other man."[14] However, this statement could be applied in various ways depending on how you define the word "infringes." For example, in order to be a consistent libertarian applying the nonaggression principle, a thick libertarian would say there should be no statements about personal morality because such statements infringe on others' equal

13. Reisenwitz, "Coercion, Persuasion, and Shaming."
14. Spencer, *Social Statics*, 74.

freedom by making them feel bad or influencing their behavior. This is why some have developed the terms "thick libertarianism," the belief that one cannot impose one's belief system on another, with or without the state's approval, and "thin libertarianism," the belief that one can impose one's beliefs on another in a personal capacity but cannot do so via the state.[15]

What does "coercion" mean? I define it to mean exerting one's will on another and achieving the desires of that will by force or threat of force. Friedrich Hayek defined it in *The Constitution of Liberty* as such: "By co-ercion we mean such control of the environment or circumstances of a person by another that, in order to avoid greater evil, he is forced to act not according to a coherent plan of his own but to serve the ends of another."[16]

Coercion in itself is not necessarily a bad thing. In normal life we allow it in certain circumstances. In libertarian circles, "coercion" has become a dirty word that people improperly and pejoratively throw around; however, if I "coerce" my three-year-old brother by stopping him from running into a busy street, that's a good thing. I have saved his life, or at least his quality of life, and therefore his liberty. As another example, once I joined three other men in preventing unwanted sexual attention from a man to a young woman on a Washington, DC Metro car. She was visibly uncomfortable as she rebuffed an attempted kiss from a stranger. Although we did not use physical force, we stepped between him and the woman as one of the bystanders verbally confronted the offender. We coerced him into exiting the metro car at his stop to end the unwanted romantic pursuits. The young woman thanked us for stepping in.

Determining whether coercion is good or bad also wholly depends on who is doing the coercing or judging and why they're doing it. God's judgment is completely justified because he is all-knowing, all-loving, and perfect in motivation.[17] The Bible is replete with accounts of his judgments. God seems to use coercion as a last resort. Had he not, we'd all be dead because of our sins.

Libertarians have a rightly skeptical and even biblical view of coercion when it comes to political judgments because people are prone to self-inter-ested actions. People are fallen, as Jacqueline Isaacs discusses in chapter 1. Human political rulers—because fallenness is a human trait—have limited

15. Johnson, "Libertarianism Through Thick and Thin."
16. Hayek, *The Constitution of Liberty*, 20–21.
17. Ps 9:8: "And he judges the world with righteousness; he judges the peoples with uprightness;" Ps 32:1–11

and imperfect knowledge, which tends to make them poor rulers and even worse economic distributors.[18] Additionally, as discussed above, their perceptions of moral behavior may be wrong and harmful to the citizens they are sworn to protect when such perceptions are turned into law.

Motivated by this real fear, libertarian discussions will erupt from time to time about judging or "shaming" (calling out bad behavior), "virtue libertarianism," and how libertarians should act toward unseemly behavior.[19] As mentioned above, some libertarians say that judging personal moral behavior is wrong in and of itself. But shaming—calling out bad behavior—is not necessarily a bad thing, either. For instance, it is perfectly legitimate to tell someone, "Don't be rude to my wife!" As with coercion, its level of acceptability depends on how it's done, who is doing it, and to whom it is addressed. There is good coercion and bad coercion.

The Bible tells us that Jesus spent time with society's moral outcasts. His message and love, not public shaming, changed their behavior. Too quickly the church can jump to public judgment when it should start with private interactions in the context of relationship. In a friendship or a close relationship with someone, I can build up respect and rapport to sit down with a friend, listen, and then share my perspective. Shaming, judging, and calling out bad behavior are not necessarily bad, but the wrong methods can have disastrous effects. There is overlap here with libertarianism, which is a political philosophy that holds that the wrong political methods can also have disastrous effects. How, then, can my Christian morality be applied in the context of political beliefs—that is, libertarianism?

Let's go back to the example of premarital sex. Premarital sex is widely taught in orthodox Christianity to be immoral. If I think it is wrong to engage in premarital sex, I can handle my encounters with that behavior in others in many different ways. I've got options! I can use my voice to speak against it in my own life, in the lives of others, to crowds of people, in books, in many other ways; or I can threaten force against those who do it; or I can be a purity vigilante of sorts and actually force people to stop, like a celibacy Batman; or I could promote government action and try to make premarital sex illegal through legislation, employing a "legal moralism," as Kevin Vallier has called it.[20] So which option should I choose? As a liber-

18. Hayek, "Use of Knowledge in Society," 519–30.

19. Gillespie et al., "Libertarianism, Yes! But *What Kind*"; Reisenwitz, "Coercion, Persuasion, and Shaming."

20. Vallier, "Opportunities for Collaboration."

tarian Christian, what is the proper response? The first option is the proper response: to speak against it, but to do so in an attitude of love and grace. As Paul expresses it, "Let your conversation be always full of grace, seasoned with salt, so that you may know how to answer everyone."[21]

In making moral judgments, Christians should have a different approach and expectation for those who profess belief in Christ than from those who do not. We shouldn't expect Christian morality or life choices from those who aren't Christians. Paul says in First Corinthians 5 that we shouldn't expect those outside our faith to behave like us. The Corinthian church seems to have been confused about his instructions because he tells them that if Christians weren't to associate with the sexually immoral, then they'd have to leave this world! It is God's job to judge those outside the church and our job to humbly follow God.[22]

In Matthew 18, Jesus tells his followers how to gently and discreetly correct a fellow *believer's* sin: "If your brother sins against you, go and tell him his fault, between you and him alone. If he listens to you, you have gained your brother. But if he does not listen, take one or two others along with you, that every charge may be established by the evidence of two or three witnesses. If he refuses to listen to them, tell it to the church. And if he refuses to listen even to the church, let him be to you as a Gentile and a tax collector."[23] Remember, Jesus still had dinner and spent time with Gentiles and tax collectors.[24] It starts with a gentle, private confrontation with the individual and, if that individual does not change his or her behavior, it works outward from there into the community. Of course, Jesus called out the sinful thoughts and actions of those he met, but he's Jesus, the God of the universe, so he can do that.

Following Jesus's example, then, whether the wrongdoer in question is a believer or nonbeliever, the person should be treated with love. Christians are given firm instructions on how to confront immoral behavior among believers but notably not how to do it among nonbelievers, of whom we shouldn't expect Christian behavior. What the Bible does seem to make clear is the Golden Rule ("So whatever you wish that others would do to you, do also to them, for this is the Law and the Prophets,"[25] which is an

21. Col 4:6
22. 1 Cor 5:9–13
23. Luke 18:15–16
24. Mark 2:13–17
25. Matt 7:12

appeal to self-interest, by the way). Judgment that is not done in love is wrong. The rule I like to keep in mind is that confrontations involving personal moral judgments about someone's private behavior should generally be avoided, since such judgments can easily be corrupted by selfish motivations and incomplete knowledge. Following the Golden Rule will lead to a much more empathetic approach that often goes much farther than an outright declaration of right and wrong.

On the other hand, it must be acknowledged that there is evidence to suggest that calling out bad behavior can create social good. The concepts of taboo and common law came from shaming. Adam Smith in *Theory of Moral Sentiments* stated, "Those general rules of conduct, when they have been fixed in our mind by habitual reflection, are of great use in correcting the misrepresentations of self-love concerning what is fit and proper to be done in our particular situation."[26] Morality and "general rules of conduct" help us to be better people. The "self-love" Smith cites refers to a myopic self-interest that would eschew any consideration of how one individual's actions might negatively affect others. Morality makes society better.

In sum, coercion in and of itself is not bad; it just depends on the circumstances and who is doing the coercing. Christians shouldn't expect those outside the church to behave like Christians do, but they should be responsible for those in the church. When it comes to judging behavior that isn't directly harmful to others, a Christian's response should be guided by the Holy Spirit, narrowly directed, and gentle.

Best of all, a libertarian system of limited government allows for the peaceful coexistence of freewheeling libertines and legalistic Christians. These two groups of people can live in peace together despite holding opposing moral worldviews. Unkindness can come from both sides, but in a system of limited government, neither group can use the state to coerce the other to behave according to its preferences and beliefs.

LIBERTARIAN CHRISTIANS

If we can make moral judgments as libertarian Christians, then why shouldn't Christian morals compel government welfare or promotion of social values in the government? Respectively, these would be the normal "social justice" and "social conservative" systems of thought. Social justice advocates often call for more government involvement in taking care of

26. Smith, *The Theory of Moral Sentiments*, 160.

the poor through welfare programs but do not advocate for laws govern-ing personal moral behavior. Social conservatives often advocate for laws to enforce personal moral behavior but do not advocate for expansion of welfare programs. Yet for both of these groups, it is in society's best interest to follow Christian moral structures. Both groups believe it's the duty of government to encourage those moral laws through legal enforcement and educational efforts such as Smokey Bear campaigns.

When it comes to issues of "social values" in regard to welfare pro-grams and personal moral behavior, libertarian Christians don't trust state coercion because easily corruptible human beings are involved. Rather, they believe in original sin, which is the theological understanding that humans are born into rebellion against God. Humans have a proclivity of varying degrees to be self-seeking and prideful. The libertarian Christian would therefore not trust error-prone humans with unaccountable and powerful political institutions.

The same distrust that results from the doctrine of human fallibility applies to moral political scenarios. Humans can easily misunderstand, mis-construe, or wield moral language to ends that are stifling to others' liberty, as with "Christian" presidential candidates who clamor for a border wall and the expulsion of immigrants. In a democracy, if a ruling majority can determine what is "moral," that determination could in fact be immoral by Christian standards. America's history has, perhaps, the most famous warning against immoral majority rule in *Federalist* 10.[27] These discussions about human fal-libility in the political sphere played an influential role in America's founding.

During high school and college, as I was forming my political philoso-phy, the reasoning seemed formulaic to me: I believe in a unifying truth, I can vote and have an active political role, and the government is supposed to carry out God's will in accordance with Romans 13 (See Jason's discussion of Romans 13 in chapter 2 for further discussion). Therefore, I should promote this unifying truth through voting and personal advocacy. My Christianity seemed to necessitate a political position on the popular social issues of the day—gay marriage, abortion, the War on Terror—whatever the cost.

Pearcey endorses this worldview and laments "secular political phi-losophies." She says:

> Perhaps the greatest tragedy is that many evangelicals in the eighteenth and nineteenth century failed to recognize what was happening. Having embraced a two-story concept of truth, they

27. Madison, *Federalist* 10.

assumed that political philosophy was a lower-story 'science' that could be pursued apart from any distinctively Christian perspective. As a result, many evangelicals at the time simply adopted secular political philosophies—especially that of John Locke. Whatever Locke's personal religious faith was (which is endlessly debated), there can be no doubt that his political theory was at root secular, grounding civil society not in moral goods like Justice and Right but merely in individual self-interest.[28]

Many Christians today think, like Pearcey, that it is the lack of overt Christian morality in the fabric of our governing laws that is our root problem. On the contrary, the separation of explicitly Christian morality from political action means good morals survive and bad ones die away. Of course, for Christians, morality is not a numbers game (see the book of Judges in the Bible for examples of a moral minority that lead while the majority were not following God's moral laws). Morality is not dependent on popular support. For instance, there is a shift in American conceptions of recreational drug use, as evidenced by the states that have passed marijuana legalization laws. Recreational drugs can certainly be abused, and the laws against their use are meant to promote a more prosperous society. There's also a moral case to be made that one should not abuse drugs. But legislative bans impact and prohibit the occasional responsible use of less dangerous drugs, namely marijuana. If a certain personal moral behavior is codified in law, there's a good chance individual liberty will decrease without society growing more moral as intended. For instance, according the US Department of Health and Human Services report, "Health, United States, 2015," illicit drug use of any type by persons over twelve-years old has increased from 8.3 percent of the population in 2002 to 10.2 percent in 2014.[29]

But all this begs the question: is the government good at promoting moral values? What is the government supposed to do when it comes to morality—or what should it do, period? When it comes to moral behavior, I think J. Budziszewski, professor of government and philosophy at the University of Texas, said it well: "It means [the state] gets out of [the true teachers of virtue's] way, and keeps other things from getting in their way."[30] What is the state good at? It specializes in enforcement and little else, as Jason explains in chapter 2. We apply a refined lens of comparative advan-

28. Pearcey, *Total Truth*, 383.

29. National Center for Health Statistics, table 50, 192.

30. Budziszewski, *The Revenge of Conscience*, 72.

tage to all our other evaluations of goods and services. Why don't we do the same with government? We don't go to Home Depot to buy groceries; we go to a grocery store. Why ask the government to do something it's not good at? It's not good at a lot of things, like arranging a weekend outing for you and your family. My position as a libertarian is that government exists to protect life, liberty, and property. Any deviation from these core principles and, particularly the infringement of any of those principles, means the government's action is unjust.

This is why I am pro-life. I believe life begins at conception, and it is the role of government to protect life. Other prominent libertarians are pro-life as well, such as former congressman Ron Paul, former Libertarian presidential candidate Bob Barr, and the libertarian-leaning Republicans currently in Congress, including Senator Rand Paul and Representatives Justin Amash, Thomas Massie, and Dave Brat. If life begins at conception, then the argument is clear that abortion, the taking of an innocent person's life, is a violation of the nonaggression principle. Murder fundamentally violates a biblical moral principle as Jesus taught, endorsing the Ten Commandments.[31]

Public policies have varying effects, but are these effects the outcomes a Christian would actually want? Say it is my desire to stamp out the immoral prostitution industry. Total eradication would require constant surveillance, ripe for abuse by those in power. Think what this would mean: in order to make sure no one is participating in prostitution, the government would need to know with certainty what everyone is doing at all times. That means the government is monstrously large and has unlimited power to squelch all prostitution whenever it wants. And if history has taught us one thing, it is that governments do not stay within their original mandate or scope of power. We've already seen the effects of a mandate to wipe out drug sales: incredibly high prison rates and innocent bystanders, including children, maimed and killed.[32] We've seen the effects of a mandate to wipe out terrorists wherever they hide: drone strikes and collateral damage. Hospitals and apartments are bombed, murdering hundreds of innocents in the pursuit of evil people. These are the heartbreaking, real-world side effects of morally inspired policy positions.

There are exceptions, however. If it's your desire to murder me, well, sorry, the government should step in and prevent that—not just because I don't like to be murdered, but because I believe that's the government's role.

31. Matthew 5:21
32. Johnson, "*Georgia Toddler in Induced Coma*," para. 1.

The government exists to protect me from your impermissible exertion of force against my life. Murder is a moral issue, and laws exist to prevent it because it is both prohibited by God and violates the nonaggression principle.

Anyone wondering whether or not the government should get involved in a question of personal morality should refer to the flow chart below.

Should the government enforce this moral behavior?

Is someone being physically harmed or killed?

YES   NO

Pass a law prohibiting it! This is government's purpose.

Is their liberty being hampered as claimed by them or any reasonable person?

YES   NO

Produce or advocate for a targeted law to prevent further infringement.

Is their property being taken or otherwise made unusable?

Produce or advocate for a *narrowly* targeted law to prevent further infringement.

YES

NO

Sorry, no laws here!

This chart illustrates the application of the nonaggression principle discussed earlier.

THE TENSION

My arguments have thus far relied on debunking misconceptions from the two sides of this issue. Some on the Christian side say Christians cannot be libertarians based on a misunderstanding that libertarians must endorse an amoral or immoral worldview, and the opposing secular libertarian side misunderstands Christianity to be *primarily* about moral rules and forced moral behavior. Libertarianism is a political philosophy that has little room for leaders or laws to compel a certain set of moral beliefs. In a libertarian context, proponents of both sides of a personal moral issue can say that the state has no role when life, liberty, and property aren't infringed. When both sides recognize what terms mean and what assumptions they're making, it can be agreed that Christians can be libertarians because libertarian does not mean libertine.

Despite all that has been said to this point, it is important to remember Christian morality will require you to do things you do not like. Christian morality may even prevent you from doing the thing you want to do most, because that thing is wrong. One excellent example of this mindset is found in Charlotte Brontë's *Jane Eyre*. After falling in love with a man she believes to be single, Jane Eyre discovers his wife is infirm but still alive, locked away from society in her husband's manor. Jane has an internal debate between her heart, which desperately wants to dive head over heels for this man, and her head and spirit, which cry foul. She concludes, "Laws and principles are not for the times when there is no temptation: they are for such moments as this, when body and soul rise in mutiny against their rigour; stringent are they; inviolate they shall be."[33]

But just because you don't like to do something doesn't make it coercion. Believing in the Christian God is a theoretically sound basis from which to make moral judgments. It requires an open-mindedness to the possibility that God has a better handle on the situation than you do. Christian living is about far more than just moral living. I surrender my life to Jesus, and from that action springs morality. Salvation is not a product of my behavior; it is not a transactional exchange. Nowhere does scripture say that I must provide *X* number of moral behaviors and then I will receive salvation. Rather, I *submit* to salvation and *X* moral behaviors are given to me. I and many others have tried unsuccessfully to live the other way

33. Brontë, *Jane Eyre*, 204. Although I read the book on my own, I must give credit to Tim Keller, pastor of Redeemer Presbyterian Church in New York City, for pointing out this particular scene.

around. It doesn't work. Instead, the Christian life starts with God's seeking us, our response, and then our living out what he's taught us. Only with this attitude can the mystery of Christian moral living be applied. Only then can it make any sense to "turn the other cheek"[34] and to give all I have to the poor.[35]

CRUCIAL QUESTIONS

This chapter is aimed primarily at Christians who have chosen to be conservative due to misconceptions about libertarian morality. But I recognize there may be readers who are not Christian but have the thick or thin libertarian perspective and seek to understand why I and other libertarians still adhere to Christian morals. Regardless of your point of view, there are still some final questions and considerations that can change your perspective and perhaps lend to more fruitful discussion.

(1) Is it at least plausible that a god could have a better ethic than you or even humanity as a whole can decide upon? Relying on our own interpretations, we can mess up a lot. God, if he exists, would indeed know the best way to live. As C.S. Lewis wrote in *Mere Christianity,* "In reality, moral rules are directions for running the human machine. Every moral rule is there to prevent a breakdown, or a strain, or a friction, in the running of that machine. That is why these rules at first seem to be constantly interfering with our natural inclinations."[36] Giving our lives to God means answering this question in the affirmative: yes, it is plausible and compelling that God has a better ethic than I or all of humanity. This question applies to the conservative Christians who seek to apply their morality in the legal sphere as well as to secular libertines. If you still think God does not exist, that's okay. But to understand where we're coming from, this point must granted credence: if the Judeo-Christian god exists, he would know the best ethic.

(2) Has God communicated those ethical rules to humanity? If we answer, yes, or even, maybe, to the previous question, then this question naturally follows. Christians say that God has communicated and communicates these rules through the Holy Spirit, the Bible, and creation, and we can interpret all of these through our reasoning abilities, granted to us by God. There are many reasons to place confidence in the scriptures and to

34. Matt 5:39
35. Matt 19:21
36. Lewis, "Mere Christianity," 65.

take them at their word. There isn't nearly the space here to give an over-view of the reasons and resources available, but a good place to start is with the resurrection of Christ. For if that can be disproven, then "we are of all people most to be pitied."[37] Any large bookstore will have sections devoted to an area of study known as Christian apologetics. If you want to know why the rules God communicates can be trusted on their merits, then I suggest some study in that field.

(3) Without God or an objective moral source, how would you deter-mine moral virtue? Perhaps you've declined to affirm either of the previous questions. That's okay! We can still be friends; I would welcome it. But if you believe there is no god, or if your stance is that all normative moral judgments are wrong, then this question must be answered. It's difficult to have a conversation with someone who eschews all manner of objective moral reasoning. For example, saying, "Normative moral judgments are wrong," is itself a normative moral judgment. See, it gets tricky. If you are an atheist, where are you getting your morality? Perhaps you may source it to evolutionary norm-setting like Hayek, which I guess is better than nothing. But then it gets tricky to argue for or against moral actions on a historical timescale, since widely accepted systems of the past, like slavery, were once considered morally good during that evolutionary stage of the societies that endorsed them.

These questions are just meant to get the juices flowing and undergird the discussion that has come before. If you are a Christian, they can be helpful in refining your own beliefs. Our beliefs should not be taken for granted but examined on their merits. If you are somewhere in between or believe in another god, then we are probably on the same page. If you are nowhere near Christian, theist, or moralist, then hopefully this provides some background on why I and many others believe what we believe.

CONCLUSION

As a libertarian Christian, my belief that someone's personal actions are wrong or right is not enforced via the state. Their actions may indeed be morally wrong, but I don't want the government to use its monopoly on force to make sure that person complies with my preferred morality. My moral judgments lack truly coercive power and should be rooted in love that ultimately comes from God's good grace. I might get that dynamic

37. 1 Cor 15:12–19

wrong by saying or doing hurtful things (God, may that never happen!) because I am a human being with limited knowledge and am inclined to selfish behavior. However, my beliefs tell me there's at least a standard out there to which I should adhere, whether or not I am always capable of doing so.

Ultimately, in determining whether personal moral behaviors are right or wrong, what matters to the Christian is that God is the supreme judge. He has perfect knowledge and is perfectly good, so he is capable of and has the right to make perfect judgments.[38]

Two quotes from very different sources adequately summarize my thoughts on this matter. In season two of my favorite TV show, *Arrested Development*, Buster Bluth, on his way to join the army, defiantly and emphatically tells his mother, who has been having an affair with his uncle: "I don't agree with your dirty doings here, but I will defend with my life your right to do them!"[39] Humankind will not always agree on what correct personal moral behavior is, but a free society requires this humble attitude and belief in others' right to live out their beliefs.

And finally, in the words of Walter Block: "My present view with regard to 'social and sexual perversions' is that while none should be prohibited by law, I counsel strongly against engaging in any of them."[40] Libertarianism as a political philosophy allows us to fully live out the lives God has planned for us as agents capable of moral behavior. As a libertarian, you can be a libertine, but that is certainly not required. As a Christian, you can be a libertarian and do not have to be a libertine.

38. "There is only one lawgiver and judge, he who is able to save and to destroy. But who are you to judge your neighbor?" (James 4:12).

39. *Arrested Development*, Episode no. 24, Directed by Patty Jenkins.

40. Block, "Libertarianism and Libertinism," 127.

BIBLIOGRAPHY

Block, Walter. "Libertarianism and Libertinism." *Journal of Libertarian Studies* 11, no. 1 (Fall 1994): 117–28.

Brontë, Charlotte. *Jane Eyre*. London: Service & Paton, 1897.

Budziszewski, J. *The Revenge of Conscience: Politics and the Fall of Man*. Eugene, OR: Wipf and Stock, 2010.

Geisler, Norman, and Frank Turek. *Legislating Morality*. Eugene, OR: Wipf and Stock, 1998.

Gillespie, Nick, W. Ruger, J. Sorens, S. Horwitz, D.N. McCloskey, and K. Mangu-Ward. "Libertarianism, Yes! But *What Kind* of Libertarianism?" *Reason*. June 9, 2016. http://reason.com/archives/2016/06/09/libertarianism-yes-but-what-kind-of-libe/.

Hayek, Friedrich. *The Constitution of Liberty*. Chicago: University of Chicago Press, 1978.

Hayek, Friedrich. "Use of Knowledge in Society." *American Economic Review* 35.4 (1945): 519–30.

Arrested Development. Episode no. 24, first broadcast 14 November 2004. Directed by Patty Jenkins and written by Mitchell Hurwitz & Jim Vallely.

Johnson, Alex. "Georgia Toddler in Induced Coma After Being Hurt by Police Grenade." *NBCNews.com*. May 30, 2014. http://www.nbcnews.com/news/us-news/georgia-toddler-induced-coma-after-being-hurt-police-grenade-n119046.

Johnson, Charles W. "Libertarianism through Thick and Thin." *Rad Geek People's Daily*. October 3, 2008 (revised July 20, 2013). http://radgeek.com/gt/2008/10/03/libertarianism_through/.

Lewis, C. S. *Mere Christianity*, in *The Complete C. S. Lewis Signature Classics*. New York: HarperCollins, 2002.

National Center for Health Statistics. *Health, United States, 2015: With Special Feature on Racial and Ethnic Health Disparities*. Hyattsville, MD: 2016.

Pearcey, Nancy. *Total Truth: Liberating Christianity from Its Cultural Captivity*. Wheaton, IL: Crossway, 2005.

Reisenwitz, Cathy. "Coercion, Persuasion, and Shaming: A Follow-Up." *Thoughts on Liberty*. September 19, 2013. http://thoughtsonliberty.com/coercion-persuasion-and-shaming-a-follow-up.

Roys, Julie, Al Mohler, and Norman Horn. "Can a Christian Be Libertarian?" *Up for Debate*. Moody Radio. March 5, 2016, radio broadcast, 46:50. http://www.moodyradio.org/Up-for-Debate/2016/2016-03-05-Can-a-Christian-be-Libertarian/.

Smith, Adam. *The Theory of Moral Sentiments*. Oxford: Oxford University Press, 1976.

Spencer, Herbert. *Social Statics: Or, the Conditions Essential to Happiness Specified, and the First of Them Developed*. London: John Chapman, 1851.

Vallier, Kevin. "Opportunities for Collaboration with Political Christians." *Bleeding Heart Libertarians*. October 21, 2015. http://bleedingheartlibertarians.com/2015/10/opportunities-for-collaboration-with-political-christians/.

4

Bards with Breadcrumbs: Optimists with a Story to Tell

Leah Hughey

There are thousands of ways to interpret the past. The one we choose will shape our expectations, our hopes, and our perceptions of the boundaries that cradle the possible. This is why, from civilization's infancy, stories have been the fabric of cultures and why we still revere the early bards who taught us to be chroniclers, historians, and poets.

Ages after those first poets, we are bards still. Over coffee, on social media, in classrooms, or leaning over the cutting board preparing dinner, we share with our chosen audiences the happenings of our days and rehash current events taking place in the wider world outside our windows. With our words, our attitudes, and the tones of our prayers, we are shaping cultural expectations that will aim the arrow of progress as it moves forward through the history books that will someday describe this age.

So why this verbose defense of history? If we are all bards, then what is required of us? Should we buy a lute and build a campfire? One may, but that isn't the point. Rather, it's simply that the way we view our lives, both present and past, massively impacts the way we view and even shape the future. If we lament, fixate on war, harp on class struggle, forecast that nothing will ever be good again, or sigh that the good old days are far behind us, then we're unlikely to explore and find any evidence to the contrary.

If we look carefully, we might see a different truth emerging. If we observe that things are actually getting better for a lot of people, then aren't we responsible for telling someone, loosening pessimism's grip, and inspiring our listeners? I think so. So consider this my attempt to explain why, as a Christian first and a libertarian second, I view the past and the future as a continuing story of hope and possibility.

This profound optimism animates my thoughts and my stories because I marvel at the ordinary wonders of market processes and astounding innovations. More than that, my Christian convictions give me hope that, even if history weren't telling a story that many people's living conditions and opportunities are rapidly improving, my hope in Christ would remain steadfast. Believing both of these realities to be compelling and beautiful, I have no choice but to live my life in light of them.

Thus, if you accept the arguments of the previous chapters, and envision yourself joining us in our declaration that libertarianism and Christianity are compatible, then this chapter is your challenge to live a life that reflects that belief. These ideas should be catalysts, whether as the narrative thread in the story you tell about the world around you or as the animating fire that leads you to launch a new career, create something, or otherwise solve a problem for yourself or for someone you love. In this age of competing stories and endless possibilities, there is too much at stake to remain silent or to sit still.

This is why the call to be a bard for optimism is so important—the future needs an advocate. As Christians, we have an ultimate hope in Christ, and as libertarians, we have an ordinary hope in our skills and abilities, our passions, and our imaginations to improve our lives and the lives of others. Our worldview, as libertarian Christians, uniquely positions us to be that advocate and to tell a story that the world should hear.

THE SORT OF TALES WE OUGHT TO TELL

One of the last century's greatest bards, J.R.R. Tolkien, told a magnificent tale centered on the astounding things ordinary people are capable of achieving when animated by an undying hope that a better, attainable future lies ahead. In the films based on Tolkien's stories, Gandalf, one of Tolkien's most memorable characters, observes that "Saruman believes it is only great power that can hold evil in check, but that is not what I have found. I've found it is the small things. Everyday deeds of ordinary folk that keeps the darkness at bay. Simple acts of kindness and love."[1]

1. *The Hobbit*, Scene 20, directed by Peter Jackson.

While he didn't intend for this observation to be a defense of Christianity or of libertarianism, Tolkien's words summarize well the synthesis point where the more subtly beautiful elements of both mingle. It is in a focus on individual people, the relationships between them, and the problems they face that we find the most fruitful tools for combating darkness and reducing suffering. One of Christianity's central commands, to love one another,[2] begins here in this interaction between individuals. Christians are also individually held accountable before God, as our actions have eternal ramifications.[3] Libertarianism, too, assumes that the individual is the central actor, from whom societies flow. It is individuals who roll up their sleeves and assist their neighbors, invent and discover cures for diseases, build businesses that offer employment and opportunity, and coordinate together to raise the standards of living for everyone.

While no amount of creativity, intellectual prowess, or material progress can solve the deeper human need for reconciliation with God through Christ, increases in quality of life, literacy, access to clean water, and lifespan are nonetheless good things. After all, this world is more than war and cancer. It also contains kindness and cures, which I believe are reflections of the nature of God. Because we are made in his image, as dimly divine little creatures, people bring about small restorations every day if we have eyes to see them.

When libertarian Christians see with both of these forms of optimism—hope in the ultimate and in the ordinary—they are more likely to trust others and to resist the fear-driven desire to control them. They are then freer to live in community with them, to love them through their challenges and mistakes, and to allow them to make decisions for themselves. And when thousands of people make decisions for themselves, within a system that coordinates the unknowable and the unfathomable, we see the sort of market progress that has driven down poverty and brought about a standard of living unseen in any other time in human history.

With a loosened grasp on the need to control and to engineer specific outcomes, libertarian Christians admit what they don't yet know. Curious and humble, they ask of the creative and the bold to run at the valley between the known and the not yet reached, throwing breadcrumbs behind them. In moments of discovery, they recall that all truth is God's truth.

2. John 13:34
3. Rom 14:12

Thus, increases in knowledge only help us to see folds of our King's heavenly robes that were yesterday obscured.

In this way, libertarian Christians live life as bards with breadcrumbs, living out the purpose God has for humankind, despite our flaws. Telling a hopeful story, we await glory with a longing that nonetheless enjoys the discovery and the creativity possible *here*, in the world we've been given, until we see our dear Savior face to face.

WHY I'M AN OPTIMIST. OR, WHY WHINERS SHOULD READ DIFFERENT NEWSPAPERS

In December 2015, as I was thinking about this chapter, I read an article in *Relevant Magazine*, called "Why You Should Be Optimistic About the Future," discussing the Christian's call to optimism.[4] While reading it, my audible cheering probably disturbed the people sitting around me. Exclamations of enthusiasm aside, the article, mixed with countless lectures, graphs, and statistics I've picked up over the last few years while studying in libertarian circles, shares a few facts that bear repeating and demand deep thought.

For starters, while it seems that we're in a constant state of war, the world since the 1970s and 1980s has seen a dramatic decline in "organized conflicts of all kinds," resulting in a major reduction in death tolls all over the world.[5] In fact, "you are less likely to die a violent death today than at any other time in human history."[6]

Even with the hyperbolic emphasis on terrorism across the globe, Americans are more likely to be killed by their own furniture than by a terrorist.[7] I'm not suggesting that you adopt hyper-minimalism as a safety measure, but I encourage you to consider the ramifications of that statistic and to avoid the popular tide of fear. We're called to do so much that we will be unable to do if we're hiding or wasting productive energies building bunkers or walls.

Global poverty is also on a sharp decrease, as the one-dollar-per-day poverty rate has declined from 26.8 percent in 1970 to only 5.4 percent in 2006.[8] From the time of my own birth in the early 1990s, the United

4. Carey. "Why You Should Be Optimistic."
5. Pinter. "Violence Vanquished."
6. Bailey. "The Decline of Violence."
7. Shaver. "You're More Likely to Be Fatally Crushed."
8. Perry. "Chart of the Greatest."

Nations reported a 21.4 percent reduction in undernourished people, in spite of the fact that we have simultaneously welcomed 1.9 billion new souls into our world in the same stretch of time.[9] Also in my own lifetime, life expectancy has globally increased from 65.3 to 71.5 years.[10]

Across the globe, wealth has been on a sharp increase over the last several centuries, and it is undeniable that humanity is much better off now than at any other historical moment. To illustrate that trend, a graph depicts the growth of wealth per person since 1000 AD.[11] While it was relatively flat for centuries, the chart tips dramatically upward in the eighteenth century, creating what resembles a hockey stick.

While multiple scholars have offered explanations to account for the obvious, sharp uptick, economist Deidre McCloskey's explanation is my personal favorite, elaborating that this surge was not brought about by purely material, economic forces. Instead, McCloskey argues that "valuations, opinions, talk on the street, imagination, expectations, hope are what drive an economy."[12] At the crux of the hockey stick's turn is actually a set of ideas that encouraged people to innovate. In McCloskey's words, "talk and ethics and ideas caused the innovation,"[13] and innovation caused the rest. Those ideas and ethics were a positive shift toward the ideas of free markets and an exceptional trust of wealthy classes (or bourgeois) that hadn't been part of culture for thousands of years.[14] In ordinary discussions and in national policy, the bards of the day came to view positively the potential of markets and the innovative forces that drive it forward, and the world changed. Libertarians universally view this shift as a major improvement for mankind.

If the newspapers you read, the academics you listen to, or even your own circles don't tell this story, that things are vastly improving, then maybe you should subscribe to a few new streams of thought. If there is some way you can change the conversation and suggest giving optimism a chance, then I challenge you to do so.

9. Food And Agriculture Organization of the United Nations. *The State of Food.*

10. GBD 2013 Mortality and Causes of Death Collaborators, "Global, Regional, and National."

11. Noell, *Economic Growth*, 7.

12. McCloskey, *Bourgeois Dignity*, 8.

13. Ibid., 6. For more explanation on this, and to see a recreation of the graph, check out Deidre's video on Learn Liberty, *What Caused The Economic Boom of Wealth?* https://www.youtube.com/watch?v=aonsKBx77EQ

14. Ibid. 7.

A THEOLOGY OF OPTIMISM: HOPE IN THE ULTIMATE AND IN THE ORDINARY

Christ as the Ultimate Source of Hope

Christians should be a very optimistic people. The Bible frequently reminds us of the hope we have, which is grounded in the person of Jesus Christ, "the founder and perfecter of our faith, who for the joy that was set before him endured the cross, despising the shame, and is seated at the right hand of the throne of God."[15] Because Christ endured the cross—the ultimate act of uniting imperfect people to a perfectly righteous God, whose justice demanded satisfaction and whose love provided it through his son—we have hope that we will be blamelessly presented to God as a fellow heir and brother with Christ. That is the only hope a Christian needs, because forgiveness and restoration to our creator satisfy the greatest need of the human condition—to be fully known, fully loved, and fully accepted by God.

Extending beyond Christ, as a ray from a perfect point, is his continuing plan for redemption, which is playing out all around us. Jacqueline Isaac's chapter outlines this plan, as she explains the four-chapter gospel. As we live in this moment, anticipating what is to come, we enjoy tastes of restoration, which are like smells coming from the kitchen on a family holiday. They're reminders that something wonderful is on its way, and the reminders themselves are pleasant and sweet. The beautiful thing to come is a union with Christ and a restoration of this fallen, broken place.

The progression from Christ's resurrection to the final restoration is, in and of itself, an optimistic view of history. There are a lot of theological debates about how Christ's return will play out and what a restoration of this world actually means. However, there is broad consensus that there is a coming day when the Lord will return, make "all things new,"[16] and resume his reign, as our "Wonderful Counselor, Mighty God, Everlasting Father, Prince of Peace."[17] Because this end is commonly believed and yearned for, all Christians should be bards proclaiming the coming of peace, hope, and renewal for all who would believe.

15. Heb 12:2
16. Rev 21:5
17. Isa 9:6

Applying a Theology of Hope

Our ultimate hope in Christ and desire to be people of optimistic faith also prepare us to endure pain and suffering. James writes that Christians should "count it all joy" when they "meet trials of various kinds" because it produces steadfastness.[18] Pain also shows us our vulnerability so that we rely on the fellowship and love of other Christians; we often learn the most about love and community when they are all we have left. And over and above our human communities, the Lord also provides to us "the peace of God, which surpasses all understanding."[19]

So even if the "hockey stick" were pointed in the other direction or if quality of life were on a sharp decline, that wouldn't lessen our hope in Christ. At its core, Christian hope isn't grounded in anything this world has to offer. In fact, Christ himself was very poor and his disciples lived in poverty and suffering and nearly unanimously met with martyrdom. To say that their lives experienced any material gain as a result of the gospel would be to completely revise history. Consequently, it is unbiblical and truly harmful to suggest that Christianity brings about material prosperity or that sufficient faith can make anyone wealthy, healthy, and blessed. This view of Christianity completely misses the beauty in the stories of martyrs, missionaries, and the faithful Christians who have died, at total peace, due to disease, poverty, or oppression.

It also misses the lesson buried in the old story of Shadrach, Meshach, and Abednego, who faced death for not bowing to King Nebuchadnezzar. When facing the flames of the furnace, in punishment for their religious devotion to the God of the Bible, they answered Nebuchadnezzar that, even if God would not deliver them, they wouldn't serve the king's gods or worship the idol he had made.[20] The faith in the "even if" scenario suggests that faith and hope, here intertwined, mean that the Christian's call to belief and to hope isn't circumstantial or based on God's direct answer to prayer to deliver us from difficult situations.[21] Instead, as a visiting minister once explained in a beautiful sermon on the subject, hope is in the character of

18. James 1:2
19. Phil 4:7
20. Dan 3:16–18
21. Allen, "Daniel 3: Realistic Faith."

a God we may not always understand.[22] In this case, of course, God did deliver them. Even if He hadn't, however, their hope was deliverance enough.

Both in pleasure and in pain, Christians have fruitful opportunities to
tell a different story. Even if circumstances don't improve, and even if wars
rage and famines spread, our hope is steadfast because God's character is
sufficient. Our responsibility doesn't end at storytelling, however, because
we have the potential to do even more. We can build, create, and restore in a
way that fulfills our purpose as human beings created in the image of God.

It is here that libertarians have so much to add to the conversation.
Libertarianism teaches that creating, building, and producing are all ways
we participate in the broader market process, which libertarians typically
believe should be left alone to the fullest extent possible. While this can't
save souls or put an ultimate salve on the problem of pain, peaceful engagement in market processes and societal institutions is a fruitful way to live
life on earth. We will address this in greater detail later on, but for now it
suffices to say that libertarianism explains and empowers some of the most
beneficial ways we can practically serve our fellow men and women. The
theological significance of this practical service, and thus of what libertarianism can better help us to accomplish, is best understood with a brief
review of what humans were created to do.

PEOPLE WITH A PURPOSE: FROM GARDENS TO SKYSCRAPERS

Christian theology begins with a creative process, which God himself
executes and deems good. From there, filling and subduing his creation
with the beneficial and the beautiful,[23] particularly to bring glory to God,
has been the calling of mankind. Scripture teaches us that we play a vital
function, from start to finish, as God's creative stewards who are actively
continuing his work. That call reaches back in time to the very first humans
and extends to the end of history, when the Lord makes "all things new."[24]

The creation account in Genesis also introduces the tension Jacqueline highlights in her chapter. Humans bear the image of God, but we're
also deeply marred by sin's curse. Thus, the work of their hands is simultaneously redemptive and destructive. That unique juxtaposition explains

22. Allen, "Daniel 3: Realistic Faith."

23. Gen 1:28

24. Rev 21:5

well the human condition but also forecasts that not everything we make will be good, as was the original creation. There are cracks in our reflections of divinity, and they can show in tragic ways.

Nonetheless, there is hope that, when we create in the image of God and for his glory, the work of our hands has redemptive power. While it can't bring about heaven on earth, it can contribute eternally to the new heavens and new earth that Christ's reign promises to bring about. A libertarian perspective also highlights the earthly benefits of work and productivity. Contributing to society, through engagement in the market and entrepreneurial discovery, has a significant impact on quality of life and opportunity for vulnerable populations.

Bringing together both Christian theology and libertarian ideas, I have an appreciation for progress and see that discoveries and creations that happen here on earth are significant. That importance is poetically etched in my mind as a shadowy outline of the wild foliage of an untamed garden, which slowly fades right into the skyscrapers of a modern cityscape.

By moving the world further toward the city lights, people's lives improve beyond that of mere survival. Engagement with beauty and with truth becomes more and more possible, as civilization progresses and we discover pieces of God's world that weren't accessible yesterday. Communities grow closer together and geography no longer divides God's people. The tribes and tongues that were always intended to be one family are brought together by commerce and cultivation. The lights are turned on across the globe, and that garden-turned-city starts to look a little bit more like home. And one day, the King will return and take with him his people and the things they made for his glory.

This image was planted in my mind when, in a freshman seminar, I read the following words: "Perhaps the most fitting symbol of the development of creation from the primordial past to the eschatological future is the fact that the Bible begins with a garden and ends with a city—a city filled with 'the glory and the honor of the nations.'"[25] Referencing Revelation 21:24–26, the author interprets a promise that those things which man creates in purity, worship, and service will eternally endure and be part of the riches of the Lord's forever kingdom. Thus, as he poetically argues, the lush and pastoral image of the Garden of Eden, in part through human action and cultivation in God's image, will become a magnificent city of light.

---

25. Wolters, *Creation Regained*, 48.

THE DAY RAND AND I PARTED WAYS

In the year leading up to my studying much more deeply the ramifications of God's creation of man and our resulting duty to create but to never forget that we ourselves are but creatures, I was heavily influenced by the works of Ayn Rand. Like many in libertarian circles, Rand was my introduction to "liberty" as I now know it. In one calendar year, I read the entirety of *We the Living, Atlas Shrugged, The Fountainhead,* and *The Night of January 16.*

In her works, I found a celebration of human potential and ambition for which I was starving. I met strong characters whose capacities seemed unlimited and almost transcendent. Yet in her praise of man, I began to see the fissures and to realize she had traded the glory of the immortal God to worship her characters instead.[26] Making men into gods, Rand's celebration of human potential that first drew me into liberty soon became a threat to my burgeoning libertarian beliefs. However, after years of wrestling, I still have a cautious respect for Rand. She helped me to understand the flaws in ideologies that seek to control human beings or surrender them to the whims of groups. In her celebration of achievement, she depicted some of the better qualities of humanity.

Rand marveled at skyscrapers, and I marveled along beside her. She described powerful heroines who were capable of ruling over business empires, and I wanted to be like them. Rand helped me to understand capitalism and its foes in a way that lingers with me. By drawing out the consequences of punishing the productive, her novels depict a narrative form argument for unfettering creative potential and avoiding envious schemes to slow down the fastest runners. When governments succeed, either in slowing the runners or in deterring their desire to run at all, the "motor of the world"[27] slows to a grinding halt and people who depended on their productive energies suffer.

Why then did we part ways? Rand's Objectivism is staunchly opposed to "mysticism," by which she means religion or a belief in the supernatural. Objectivism denies that it is possible to both use reason and remain a Christian. Speaking through John Galt, the central protagonist in *Atlas Shrugged,* she doesn't make this assessment subtly. In his famous speech, Galt calls the mystic "a parasite in spirit, who plunders the ideas created by

---

26. Allusion to Romans 1:23
27. Rand, *Atlas Shrugged,* 617.

others—so he falls below the level of a lunatic who creates his own distortion of reality."[28] Some of Galt's other critiques of religion are even stronger, demonstrating Rand's overall distaste for anyone who bows in worship to any god other than man.

Rand's universe leaves no space for anything that exists above and beyond it. There is nothing above a human being and his own values, allowing for no divine spark. All is just steel and bones. This left out an important piece, which is the source of man's unique reason and creative faculties. It is not in spite of God that we create, but rather we build because his attributes dwell within us and motivate us to create bridges, skyscrapers, business empires, works of art, poetry, music, and every other worthy endeavor. Stopping at the creation misses the Creator who stands behind it and proclaims that it is good.

My resulting belief system permits me to stand on the top floor of a skyscraper, observing the blur of traffic and the endless miles of surrounding achievement with the same awe I feel at the sight of storm clouds rolling over rocky peaks. And when men and women cure disease, make prosthetics for children with a 3D printer, and employ thousands of people who sustain their families on the profits of business empires, I celebrate those achievements because of what they reflect and what they inspire, a glimmer of the Eternal City and of its King.

A BROADER VIEW OF GLORY: VALUE IN EVERY ENDEAVOR

Libertarians typically rely on the market to send a signal of the value of a job or a product, even when it doesn't necessarily cohere with our personal preferences or more subjective values. They also respect the ability of different professions to contribute to the larger market, which relies on vastly distributed resources coming together spontaneously and beneficially in a system that isn't coordinated from on high.[29] Thus, libertarians don't observe some sort of sacred versus secular division between some jobs that explicitly help people—like social work or ministry—and others that don't. By virtue of deriving a profit, which is essentially a vote of thanks or confidence in a firm for creating something beneficial, a job is implicitly valuable.

28. Rand, *Atlas Shrugged*, 957.

29. For a fuller explanation of F.A. Hayek's analysis of "spontaneous orders," see my section called "Giving Spontaneity a Try."

Christians don't always observe the same standard. Some may believe ministers and missionaries are more vocationally holy than a businessman. However, as we see in the Gospels, Jesus worked as a carpenter and, between ministry opportunities, Paul was a tentmaker. As theologian Wayne Grudem remarks, this shows "that an occupation of producing and selling goods from the earth is not in itself 'greedy' or 'materialistic,' but something that is right and pleasing in the sight of God."[30] Paul explains, in Second Thessalonians 3, that he and his followers "did not eat anyone's bread without paying for it, but with toil and labor we worked night and day, that we might not be a burden to any of you. It was not because we do not have that right, but to give you an example to imitate."[31] Paul thought earning his own way, participating in commerce to support himself, was exemplary and the way other believers should behave. He didn't participate begrudgingly in the market or view commerce as a necessary evil but rather recognized exchange as an important part of life on earth.

Some interpretations of Paul's occupation explain that this commercial activity was only intended to support his ministry, and so work is fruitful only when it results in charitable giving or religious activity. However, elsewhere in scripture, we observe responsible wealth production as a good unto itself. For instance, Matthew 25 tells the famous parable of the talents. In this parable, Jesus illustrates that it matters how we invest what we've been given, regardless of our abilities or circumstances. Though the amounts of money each servant had been given to invest varied, the expectation common to all of them was that they would produce a return.

That call to productivity isn't couched in language of charity or resulting service to the church; it simply stands that making good use of resources is virtuous and pleasing to God. This is of course the biblical concept of stewardship. When explaining stewardship, Wayne Grudem elaborates that, beyond the basic prohibition against using resources "wastefully or abusively," Christians should see the process of production itself "as something morally good."[32] Grudem continues that "God placed in the earth resources that would enable man to develop much more than food and clothing."[33] Thus, as a part of our humanity, we are called to create things as lovely and diverse as the resources we have at our disposals. There is

30. Grudem, *Politics According To The Bible*, 270.
31. 2 Thes. 3: 7–9
32. Grudem, *Politics According To The Bible*, 123.
33. Ibid., 123.

nothing inherently evil or materialistic about this process. In fact, in First Corinthians 10, Paul tells us to "do all to the glory of God," even eating and drinking. If the way we eat our food can bring God glory, then surely the way we create in his image is an opportunity for worship.

We should be cautious, then, in condemning commercial activities as less valuable than directly religious vocational callings. Brian Walsh and Richard Middleton, authors I also read in my freshman seminar course, explain this as dualism. A dualistic worldview, or one "split into two realms" between the spiritual and the secular, implies a hierarchy among careers in Christendom.[34] The danger is that we will perceive spiritual activities as so separate from our careers that we forget the Lord has dominion over everything. The authors elaborate that "the problem isn't that the Christian community is lacking in doctors, farmers, business people, or musicians. The problem is that there are so few Christian doctors, farmers, business people, and musicians."[35] With this false separation, it is difficult to imagine that we would create things worthy of laying at the Father's throne or to think sustainably about how our careers impact others.

The full tragedy of this separation comes about when we forget the significance of the people we work with and for. Everyone in society is in some way affected by the work we do and the things we create, because our creative endeavors signal to and participate in the market process. But even more directly, C.S. Lewis reminds the thoughtful Christian that "it is immortals whom we joke with, work with, marry, snub, and exploit . . . Next to the blessed Sacrament itself, your neighbor is the holiest object presented to your senses."[36] Thus, our conversations over the water cooler, the way we treat those we manage, and the reasons for which we toil at all are a ministry in and of themselves. Given "the load, or weight, or burden of my neighbor's glory," there can be no way to view our actions in the commercial realm, or any other, as anything but sacred.[37]

While there are likely thousands of accounts from which we can draw exceptional examples of this thinking applied to a "secular" vocation, the one that has most inspired me is the story of John D. Rockefeller. Historian Burt Folsom tells the story of Rockefeller's life, part of a contemporary

---

34. Walsh, *The Transforming Vision*, 97.

35. Ibid., 97.

36. Lewis, *The Weight of Glory*, 45–46.

37. Ibid.

"cloud of witnesses,"[38] demonstrating a path on earth that chases after glory in full recognition of the eternity present in every action and interaction.

Rockefeller is cited as one of history's notable "robber barons," (though this negative term doesn't at all reflect who he actually was,) known for his magnificent wealth and productivity. Beneath the superficial accounting of his ledger book, Rockefeller hoped to provide the best source of light in the world and at the lowest possible price so as to make electricity accessible for everyone.[39] Folsom recounts that "millions of Americans illuminated their homes with Standard Oil for one cent per hour; and in doing so, they made Rockefeller the wealthiest man in American history."[40] Suddenly, working class people all over America had access to sustainable light sources after dark. Previously, candles and lamp oils were prohibitively expensive, leaving the vulnerable in the dark.[41] That is until Standard Oil lit the night.

As should be the case in a free market, the service came before the fortune. Recognizing the objective value of the improvement Standard Oil brought about in the quality of life for millions of people, Rockefeller knew his business was creating a real benefit. Beyond that, by conducting himself honorably and in keeping with his Christian convictions, Rockefeller was living out the Christian call to be salt and light. Matthew 5 reminds Christians that we are "the light of the world."[42] It is poetically ironic that this passage goes on to say that a light, when placed in a spot where it has the opportunity to cast a glow all around, "gives light to all in the house."[43]

In addition to providing this vital, practical service, Rockefeller also gave away $550,000,000 over his lifetime, which was amazingly a sum larger "than any other American before him had ever possessed."[44] What did that fortune provide? Rockefeller's legacy built churches and schools, sustained global missions, and even paid for the scientific research that cured hookworm, meningitis, and yellow fever.[45] Like the parable's servants with two and five talents, respectively, who each doubled his original investments,

38. Heb 12:1
39. Folsom, *The Myth of the Robber Barons*, 83.
40. Ibid., 83.
41. Ibid., 87.
42. Matt 5:14
43. Matt 5:15
44. Folsom, *The Myth of the Robber Barons*, 97–99.
45. Ibid.

Rockefeller was a "good and faithful servant."[46] His contributions were valuable both for the way he conducted his business and in the way he gave of its fruits. Consequently, the whole house around him was illumined by the light, which he refused to hide.

Light is something our present age mostly takes for granted, but the necessity of light is most keenly observed in its absence. Satellite images of the world show a vibrant and glowing South Korea, with cities and civilization blazing and humming with life. However, nighttime in North Korea is a desolate blackness. Because of long-standing controls on the use of electricity, North Koreans use 660 kilowatt hours per person, per year. Just over the border, in South Korea, that number is over ten thousand.[47] Without Rockefellers to light the way, to toss behind them breadcrumbs to those who would follow, people needlessly live in the dark.

GIVING SPONTANEITY A TRY: A UNIFIED VIEW OF NATURAL ORDERS, MARKET PROCESSES, AND A CULTURE OF FREEDOM

Spontaneous Order

Like Rockefeller, and many others before and after him, we should be pilgrims in this world but pilgrims who nonetheless dearly love those with whom we share it. Part of our love ought to be contributing in any way we can to lessening their physical and contextual challenges so survival isn't an all-consuming exercise. Alleviating the burdens of our fellow men removes the weight from their backs, allowing them to look upward and see the majesty of the God who created rivers and who created, through us, the processes needed to make their waters safe to drink.

Thus, as libertarian Christians, we should celebrate stories like Rockefeller's as examples of people who invested the talents given to them and brought about a surge in quality of life for many people. However, we can't laud this sort of progress without simultaneously fighting the temptation to condemn the technologies and institutions that have made discoveries and surges in quality of life possible.

Appreciation for the results of those institutions necessitates a respect for the spontaneous processes that produce creative and amazing products

46. Matt 25:23
47. World Bank, *Electric Power Consumption.*

115

and ideas that advance human potential. Even if we can't fully grasp or explain how markets communicate or cultural institutions solidify, we can still marvel at the way it all works out into beautiful, aggregated systems, which have "resulted not from human design or intention but spontaneously."[48]

That is the nature of "spontaneous order," as articulated by Friedrich Hayek, who defends spontaneous or "extended" order as a result of "certain traditional and largely moral practices" of human cooperation. He later writes that spontaneous orders "enabled [people] to be 'fruitful, and multiply, and replenish the earth, and subdue it.'"[49] This allusion is not an indication that Hayek was a Christian (he was not). He also didn't credit the design of the systems behind human and market cooperation as divinely orchestrated, though I may hazard to say they are, but he does credit extended orders as the main driving force behind civilization. He goes on to argue:

> We make constant use of formulas, symbols, and rules whose meaning we do not understand and through the use of which we avail ourselves of the assistance of knowledge which individually we do not possess. We have developed these practices and institutions by building upon habits and institutions which have proved successful in their own sphere and which have in turn become the foundation of the civilization we have built up.[50]

While price systems or markets for goods and services are the most commonly cited spontaneous orders, they aren't the only examples. Anytime there is an evolutionary or progressive movement, particularly in culture or in knowledge, Hayek would argue a spontaneous order is afoot, with the telltale sign being the absence of deliberate planning. Consequently, these can be social movements that arise quickly in response to current events or even the unstoppable spread of an idea or belief system. A beautiful example is the spread of the gospel in early Christianity, as recorded in the book of Acts. After Christ issued the great commission, "Go therefore and make disciples of all nations, baptizing them in the name of the Father and of the Son and of the Holy Spirit, teaching them to observe all that I have commanded you,"[51] the gospel spread like wildfire through individual men and women telling about what they had seen.

48. Hayek, *The Fatal Conceit*, 6.
49. Ibid., 6
50. Hayek, "The Use of Knowledge," para. 25.
51. Matt. 28:19–20

Christianity encountered early opposition, climaxing in the martyr-dom of Stephen, which unexpectedly and unpredictably took the gospel to new continents that never would have welcomed early disciples and the story of Jesus. The people on the ground responded quickly to news of the martyr, spreading out in an effort to protect early believers and keep alive the story of Christ.[52] In this same way, every day, we respond to new infor-mation and do our best to carry out the purposes we feel called to both in ultimate and in ordinary circumstances. As we try to make plans, new in-formation and new events constantly confound us or signal that we should go in another direction. When we're permitted to engage and cooperate with each other, those signals are most beneficial and we're best able to execute on the purposes we have set out to achieve.

The Knowledge Problem

In addition to spontaneous order, Hayek's writings on economics also introduce us to "the knowledge problem," which explains that the data or information we all need to make even the smallest decisions doesn't exist in one place. Instead, "dispersed bits of incomplete and frequently contradic-tory knowledge" exist with the billions of individuals on our planet.[53] Every person has information that is useful to others and that somehow relates to their decision-making. Consequently, if someone were to try to make deci-sions on behalf of another person, they would necessarily miss some of their "knowledge of time and place," which only individuals can know.[54]

Taking to heart the implications of the knowledge problem, it starts making a lot of sense that many libertarians are (or should be) humble people. When you acknowledge the vastness of what you do not and cannot know and when you realize that you rely on the knowledge of millions of other people on a daily basis, you gain an acute awareness of your reliance on others and the finitude of your own understanding. Christianity also teaches its followers to be humble in the realization of the vastness of the universe in comparison to the brevity of their lives and the limits of their abilities. This teaches us to approach the universe and the mysteries therein

52. Acts 8:1.
53. Hayek, "The Use of Knowledge," para. 3.
54. Hayek, "The Use of Knowledge," para. 9.

with wonder. The processes that coordinate human knowledge are certainly a wondrous mystery, one Hayek himself calls a "marvel."[55]

While I won't claim that this is a perfect or baptized system worthy of our worship and reverence, it is miraculous in its own way. With the Internet providing plentiful customers for people who can make or do things other people want, the potential for anyone to start a business has never been higher. Well before the technological innovations of the last few decades, however, the jobs and opportunities created by profitable business have been the way people make money and care for their families. While we don't ordinarily credit the private sector with charity, this process is singularly responsible for bringing millions out of poverty and for providing nearly endless opportunity.

Market processes also channel the innate desire within us all to serve our own ends, often cited by economists as our "rational self-interest," to do things which help other people. This may be deliberate, but it is actually not often deliberate at all. Instead, workers labor because they want to be paid. They don't think charitably about the people who will consume their creations. In fact, the very first economist, Adam Smith, famously penned, "it is not from the benevolence of the butcher, the brewer, or the baker, that we expect our dinner, but from their regard to their own interest. We address ourselves, not to their humanity but to their self-love, and never talk to them of our own necessities but of their advantages."[56]

Thus, the market isn't a moral system, but it nonetheless moralizes, or at least civilizes, undeniable elements of human nature. The butcher provides a meal to a family not out of the goodness of his own heart, but because he needs to feed his own family. Those needs coalesce, but so do the incentives to treat each other with respect and honesty. If the butcher cuts inferior meat or makes someone sick, he will easily go out of business. Consequently, the market takes the bit of us that wants what's best for us and applies that to the needs of others, rewarding us for a job well done and harnessing any part of us that would prefer an easier way out. Thus, the market, when left free, has its own self-cleansing mechanism for unethical or dishonest business practices.

55. Hayek, "The Use of Knowledge," para. 23–24.
56. Smith, The Wealth of Nations, 23–24.

Being a Libertarian Is a Risky Business

Nonetheless, trust in spontaneous and free systems demands of us a heightened risk tolerance, knowing that sometimes what we create may at first appear dangerous, either in terms of risk or possible consequences, or even obscene. Initially, the risks in an entrepreneurial, free economy are primarily that competition is constantly on the move. This is excellent for the consumer, who will continue to buy better and better products for less money, but it is difficult for the businesses that lose. Naturally, this leads to temporary unemployment and other powers of creative destruction. In a free market system, however, those painful effects don't last for very long.

Spending a moment on the cultural side, I also believe Christians should be more optimistic in the face of culture and creative expression. It is easy and common to interpret, among others, the verse, "Do not be conformed to this world, but be transformed by the renewal of your mind, that by testing you may discern what is the will of God, what is good and acceptable and perfect,"[57] as a call or invitation to broadly judge the world and the culture of the age one lives in. It's tempting to believe, and to find potential biblical justification, for thinking the world is going to hell in a handbasket. However, I would challenge, once again, that the whiners should seek other sources of entertainment. Yes, culture is loud, and it does provide a lot of temptation and distraction. Yet, the point of Romans 12:2 is to suggest the renewal of one's mind and the discernment needed to make wise, personal decisions about how we engage with the world around us. Yet if every piece of art or act of culture were pure and noble, then this discernment would never form. Consequently, the larger call of the libertarian Christian is to allow for the free flow of ideas and expression, while gracefully and graciously living in contrast to what we observe that stands in contradiction to our values. Beauty, much like justice, is most visible through comparison to its opposite.

The Great Bard Under Attack

As a thought experiment, let's think for a moment about the world if we were to decide not to largely trust and rely on spontaneous orders to direct even culture. If we were to, instead, attempt to control the direction of culture, what would that look like? I agree completely with Taylor Barkley,

---

57. Rom 12:2

who earlier explained that the church shouldn't fear culture, or, heaven forbid, try to use the state to restrict it. As a means of illustrating this point, let's take a trip through history to discuss the great bard himself, William Shakespeare.

In Elizabethan England, the Puritans were known for their opposition to theater. This Puritan moment hit its peak during the Commonwealth, only decades after the works of Christopher Marlowe and William Shakespeare were written. Even though we laud them today, the Puritans viewed playwrights and their players as idle beggars who produced nothing valuable. Furthermore, the content of their plays was deemed too sexual and potentially damaging to female virtue.[58] For these reasons, among others, the Puritans shut down England's theaters in 1642. Among them, they closed the Globe Theater, which had a generation earlier become famous for debuting Shakespeare's plays.

To suggest that losing to history the works of either playwright would be a tragedy is a dramatic understatement. While it is obvious that their works survived, the broad attempt at censoring theatrical arts might have prevented the preservation of their works—a chilling thought to any lover of literature.

Yet, to suggest that one would be able to distinguish, among a crowd of playwrights, the Marlowes and Shakespeares from the purely vile and obscene is surprisingly difficult. Because both writers dealt with mature——and even lude—content intended to amuse and even mildly scandalize audiences, both provide plenty of obscene elements. Shakespeare's plays are also remembered for referencing, with disrespect, political and other leaders of his day. Thus, on grounds of treason or of obscenity, there may have been legitimate, moral grounds for halting Shakespeare's pen. And although there are undeniably objective standards of beauty, which render totally different the needlessly profane and the lovely, any sort of restriction still relies on a person (or group) to make that subjective determination. To whom would you entrust such a great responsibility and power?

American jurisprudence depicts an example of how difficult it actually is for people in positions of power to decide what should and shouldn't be restricted. In *Jacobellis v. Ohio,* a Supreme Court case on the First Amendment, which addressed pornography, Justice Stewart's concurrence famously stated: "I shall not today attempt further to define the kinds of material I understand to be embraced within that shorthand description

---

58. Morgan, Edmund S. "Puritan Hostility to the Theater," 341.

[hard pornography], and perhaps I could never succeed in intelligibly doing so. But I know it when I see it."[59] And that is the whole point, Justice Stewart: we all do. If individuals make what I would deem poor decisions in their consumption, then they must have the freedom to do so. Consequently, restricting the production of what makes us uncomfortable isn't well placed in a free society that leaves wide open the door for individuals to judge the merits of cultural materials and to steer clear of what is ugly. Somewhere, hidden among the junk and the nonsense, there may be another Marlowe or a Shakespeare. For those able to pick out those pearls, the treasure is worth the hunt.

Toward a Greater Trust in Human Potential

The culmination of our review of spontaneous order, the knowledge problem, and the gravity of attempting to legislate morality is a greater respect for individual people and their rights to make their own decisions. This doesn't just apply in market transactions but also in the ways in which they live their lives. Governed by our own consciences or by the Holy Spirit, Christians shouldn't pattern their lives after those they see around them. However, they also don't have a righteous duty to condemn, especially through force of law, that which they don't like. When there are true violations of the codes of the community, particularly when someone harms another person or commits fraud within a market, then that individual should naturally be held accountable and punished for those actions. The punishments for those violations should be decided with similar care.

As individuals become freer, norms and rules regarding behavior actually become even more important. So it isn't a fair depiction of a free society, or of the libertarian vision, to suggest that we wouldn't expect sin or be able to identify it when it arises. Instead, libertarian Christians acknowledge that offense, defamation, and destruction have been the unfortunate shadow of our natures since sin first entered the world. Regardless of the fences we place around ourselves, such will continue to be our plight until Christ returns. In the meantime, force has never succeeded in changing hearts; it has only stopped them from beating.

Yet paired with the darker sides of our natures, all humans also have the creative and redemptive element we've already discussed. If we view that as a common grace, as even those who don't call on the name of Christ

59. Jacobellis, 378 US at 184.

are capable of creating beautiful and beneficial things, we can enjoy the fruits of their production as a good gift. While there is theological debate on the eternal worth of those things created for reasons other than God's glory, there is at least temporal value for those things that advance quality of life or some other value of life here on earth.

So what are we to trust people to do, unrestrained by government direction or oversight? Because of the profit motive earlier discussed and the incentive that serves to get entrepreneurs into the ring to compete for that profit, entrepreneurs and savvy engineers can solve problems that meet needs in a way that competes with governments and can better solve people's problems.

As an easy and almost comic example, UPS and FedEx are infinitely more pleasant to work with and dependable than is the United States Postal Service. Residents in Washington, DC, New York, and other major cities can also testify to how much better Uber and Lyft are than unionized taxicabs. Private companies, like Sheetz, which is headquartered in my hometown, regularly decide to raise wages without being told to do to so by minimum wage legislation.[60]

Private, competitive policing is also on the rise, with twenty million security guards working all over the world. This is nearly double the number of government police.[61] And in the slums of Nairobe, in Mathare to be exact, there are only four public schools, despite the half million people who live there.[62] In conditions of extreme poverty, where children have presumably no shot at an education or a future, 120 private schools have moved into Mathare to provide education for as little as $1 per week.[63] While the costs are higher in the United States, many believe falsely that public education accounts for an overwhelming majority of America's educational services. However, over one quarter of the schools in the United States are private, accounting for over 30,000 different schools with unique missions and perspectives for families to choose from.[64]

Another basic need is met in America, and in many places around the world, by the much maligned and misunderstood McDonald's. People are starting to notice what Jeffrey Tucker has been saying for a while—that

60. Addady, "Sheetz Is About to Make."
61. Huemer, *The Problem of Political Authority*, 326.
62. *The Economist*. "The $1-a-Week School." August 1, 2015.
63. Ibid.
64. National Center for Education Statistics, "Fast Facts."

McDonald's offers around one thousand calories for $1.76.[65] While it isn't made of fresh vegetables from an organic garden, McDonald's food packs in a lot: around half a day's requirements for protein, 20 percent of daily calcium, and 7 percent of daily fiber in one double cheeseburger.[66] Given the comparative costs of healthier alternatives, McDonald's has the potential to keep people going who may otherwise struggle to afford sufficient calories and basic nutrition. While it may be trendier to criticize McDonald's and the pervasive presence of their golden arches, those arches now mean that many, many people can get a square meal for a pittance. With market competition, the potential exists for other rapid service restaurants to provide higher quality food for a comparable, or even lower, cost. Who knows what $1.76 could eventually buy.

Beyond these examples, it's also inspiring to look through the lists of ideas on crowdfunding sites that welcome total strangers to give money toward ideas or causes in which they believe. Whether it's paying for the medical bills of sick children, funding repairs and restorations after natural disasters, or helping people with creative ideas to have sufficient funds to launch, crowdfunding totally removes the middlemen and regulations standing between ordinary people and extraordinary solutions. Without waiting to dance through the hoops needed to secure a loan or wait for reimbursement from government-subsidized insurance, crowdfunding allows people to sympathize, with their hearts and their wallets.

In addition to crowdfunding, crowdsourcing solutions to problems is a new and emerging method of getting together brilliant, charitable minds to take a crack at some of the toughest problems of our age. The most beautiful example I've come across is E-Nable, a nonprofit started when, in 2011, founder Ivan Owen made an artificial hand for a costume. A YouTube video of his costume made it to a man in South Africa, named Richard, who asked for a hand like it, since he had lost his fingers in an accident. They collaborated on a hand for Richard, and news spread quickly.[67] In a lovely stroke of spontaneous order, there are now thousands of volunteers who work in the E-Nable community to create 3D-printed hands for children. E-Nable estimates that they've so far officially made about 1,500 hands, but they use open source software, which encourages spontaneous orders to take the designs beyond their efforts and make even more. Consequently,

65. Smith, "The Greatest Food in Human History."
66. Ibid.
67. "About Us," Enabling The Future.

123

the total count could be higher. Coming in at around $35 per hand, plus labor, this is a drop in the ocean of the $6,000 to $10,000 a prosthetic hand normally costs.[68] Typical prosthetics also have to go through the complex labyrinth of the insurance system, whereas E-Nable and its supporters give these hands directly to the children who need them. And while this is just one example of the beauty that is possible when individuals are free to collaborate toward productive ends, there are undoubtedly hundreds, if not thousands, of other groups of people across the world working together to redeem little bits of what is broken.

In this way, we can all be entrepreneurs. One doesn't have to build a business empire to innovate or to solve real problems for other people. All of us, in some small way, can dive into the valley of the unknown and attempt to learn something that will benefit others, through untold and unpredictable spontaneous processes. Those processes are the breadcrumbs we leave behind, as bards blazing our own trails and learning how to make our lives better and, hopefully, a few other lives too. This is the way libertarian Christians can most beneficially and actively engage with the knowledge problem. In the full humility of acknowledging all that we don't know and can't possibly solve on our own, libertarian Christians can encourage, fund, and participate in these innovations, and improve the already hopeful outlook most people should have about their lives on earth.

AVOIDING THE TEMPTATION TO REGULATE AWAY PROGRESS

With all of these beneficial and beautiful things coming out of the charitable and private sectors, what is the proper response from the public sector? Libertarianism teaches that the proper response from governments is to get out the way and warns that the temptation to plan, rather than to trust spontaneous orders, has long been a motivation of executive departments and Congress alike.

In the words of Virginia Postrel, a classy optimist who cases a very convincing view of the future, we can "crave predictability, or relish surprise," among a host of other juxtapositions between what she calls "stasis" and "dynamism."[69] Postrel outlines two postures with which we can look at the future, particularly from a lens of policy. One is to view future production

68. Ibid.

69. Postrel, *The Future and Its Enemies*, xiv.

as a wonderland of potential for all of us, and the other is to writhe in fear of what might happen if someone knowledgeable and cautious isn't at the helm. But, as we glean from Hayek's knowledge problem, the sort of data that would lend a planner the ability to do this just doesn't exist. Thus, Hayek's enduring legacy, which has become a pillar of libertarian thought, is a vigilant skepticism of planning schemes that cannot keep pace with the reality of constantly changing conditions and vastly distributed information.

Regardless, special interest groups, lobbying entities, and unions work to try to keep competitive newcomers out of old, nearly monopolized markets. Uber, Lyft, and other ride-sharing services have faced many a day in court from taxicab unions. Teachers' unions have fought viciously to keep away private competition. AirBnB is also effectively illegal in some cities and the state of New York, preventing homeowners from making their private property available for rent to those who would willingly pay for a place to stay.

Beyond these efforts to keep away innovators who might threaten entrenched businesses, regulations have also made the barriers to entry so high for some fledgling industries that it isn't even worth trying to build a new endeavor. Several of these threats are occupational licensing, high taxation and complex tax laws, business filing requirements, employment law surrounding new hires and growing teams, and raw regulations that present thousands of misdemeanor and criminal charges for unknowable "crimes" that we probably all commit, without realizing it, on a daily basis.

One example of such "crimes" is violation of burdensome occupational licensing laws, which prevent people from using their gifts and talents in a way that serves other people and provides for their needs. If it's truly criminal for an interior decorator, hair braider, or massage therapist to practice a trade without countless hours of unnecessary and expensive training toward a piece of paper to hang on the wall, then we are likely all criminals for not carrying cards and certifications for every piece of our own jobs. This is clearly ridiculous, and groups like the Institute for Justice fight court cases every day to overturn unnecessary regulations that prevent ordinary people, particularly in low- and moderate-income jobs, from making a living.

However, the lobbying interests that represent groups of licensed professionals have a strong interest in fighting it out and keeping others away from the profits their clients gain in their exclusive groups, and so the cycle will continue until someone stops it. The same logic applies here as it does to unions: when you can coalesce and keep others away from your market through the power of government, why wouldn't you want to take advantage of that?

High rates of taxation on small businesses as well as the burdensome process of filing taxes are also a hindrance to entrepreneurial ventures and small businesses. Filing quarterly, picking the right status, and keeping track of all of your own expenses are only a few of the staggering requirements for filing taxes as a small business entity. It almost absolutely requires a professional accountant whose main business is built upon helping other businesses navigate complex tax codes and filing structures. If such professionals didn't exist, countless more businesses would have to shut down due to genuine errors and easy mistakes in owners' documentation. However, this doesn't only apply to tax codes.

Filing for status as a nonprofit, an LLC, or any other status also requires very careful attention to detail and nearly expert knowledge of what those statuses mean and the implications for any future endeavor. On top of that, once you begin hiring employees, your legal burdens and liabilities grow considerably as your staff does. Consequently, employment law and human resources teams are a nearly essential part of a company that expands beyond a few people. With that sort of overhead existing beyond a certain point of growth, it's understandable that some business owners would choose to peak early rather than push through to a layer of complexity and growth they can't afford to sustain.

Over and above these specific examples is a growing theme of over-regulation across industries and endeavors. If we value productive energy and creativity applied to solving problems people face, then we should hate the regulatory frameworks that threaten that progress. As a snapshot of what federal regulations cost the American economy, we lost $1.88 trillion to regulations and interventions in 2014, according to the Competitive Enterprise Institute.[70] CEI elaborates that, if this were the economy of a small country, it would be the tenth largest economy in the world.[71] When you think of what the private market could have done with that money back in their pockets, it's a staggering and sickening loss. And while it isn't distributed this way, CEI calculates that this is equivalent to almost $15,000 per American household.[72]

70. Crews, Clyde Wayne. "Ten Thousand Commandments 2015."
71. Ibid.
72. Ibid.

Beyond these costs, the sheer number of federal regulations is also difficult to comprehend. According to the Regulatory Studies Center at George Washington University, there were fewer than 23,000 pages in the code of federal regulations in 1960. In 2014, that number was up to over 175,000.[73] Of the regulations on those pages, some 300,000 unique regulations are estimated conservatively to carry criminal penalties.[74] In almost every case, people have no idea they're committing criminal offenses in their everyday lives because the laws governing their behavior are so obtuse and complicated that not even an attorney whose job is exclusively devoted to understanding new regulations—and their penalties and ramifications— could possibly keep up.

Given these costs and disproportionate penalties, why do government actors still seek to regulate activity that has such a high likelihood of generating positive outcomes? As we discussed already, the two primary motivations are fear, or a desire to control, and protectionism, a strong incentive to keep out competition from growing and profitable industries when entrenched professionals don't want to welcome in a new guy who might put them out of business.

The unknown is one of the most fundamental fears of the human condition. As Postrel argues, we fear what we don't know, and that makes us want control.[75] Government officials have long promised to face the scary uncertainties for their electorates, asking only for their votes in exchange. Or, in Postrel's words, "they promise to make the world safe and predictable, if only we will trust them to design the future, if only they can impose their uniform plans."[76]

One major example is FDR's Second Bill of Rights, including a promise that he would protect the people's "right to adequate protection from the economic fears of old age, sickness, accident, and unemployment."[77] These beasts of uncertainty plague the minds and dreams of most grown adults in the way that monsters and spiders frighten children. If a politician can harness that fear, and promise to alleviate it, it takes a strength of will to turn from that and think for a moment of the costs and the impossibility of fulfilling such a promise. We would rather just believe.

73. "Reg Stats," Regulatory Studies Center.
74. Malcolm, John. "Criminal Law and the Administrative State."
75. Postrel, *The Future and Its Enemies*, 216.
76. Ibid.
77. Roosevelt, "State of The Union Message to Congress."

Beyond the financial burden, what does it actually cost to uphold a regulatory state of the size and scope we have in America today? What does it take to enforce these rules? What does it require to truly guarantee jobs, provision in old age, and protection against accidents? The answer is the defining element of all governments: the use of force to punish people until they comply with the regulations and heavy taxes. Going back to the definition we use throughout this book, libertarians are "concerned solely with the proper use of force."[78] Thus, a government's use of force to enforce regulations strikes at the heart of libertarian beliefs.

If your calculus is that regulations ultimately protect people from each other or from themselves, then throw in the moral complexity that police and jail sentences enforce those preferences you may have for a different kind of world. If you're not willing to be the one to nail the door closed on a hair braider's business, to imprison a baker for accidental errors in his taxes, or to level heavy penalties against those who don't want to pay substantial taxes into a social security system they know won't exist for them, then maybe you should think twice before approving that power to be used by those who represent you. Jason's chapter highlights this moral dilemma, specifically with a quote by Yale law professor Stephen Carter, who you may recall tells his first year students "never to support a law they are not willing to kill to enforce."[79]

I fear that more, from a moral standpoint, than I fear what may happen if regulations loosen across industries. I'm more fearful of the growing criminalization of accidental and nonviolent crimes than I am of a firebrand barber or a founder of a startup who chooses the wrong tax filing code. If you're on the side of history that values progress, particularly as it has the potential to lift the poorest and to give them opportunities to create value and beauty for themselves and for society, then you may want to consider adopting a similar calculus. I believe libertarians ought to be on that side of history. Referring back to Jason's definitions, outlining libertarians as those who only justify force for "defense or retaliation,"[80] then there really is no other option.

As Christians, it is imperative to view excessive laws and regulations as threats to our calling as peacemakers. Jesus himself taught us that

78. Block, "Libertarianism vs. Libertinism."
79. Carter," Law Puts Us All In Same Danger."
80. Block, "Libertarianism vs. Libertinism."

"blessed are the peacemakers, for they shall be called sons of God."[81] The New Testament teaches that we should seek peace first, as an outpouring of the peace and acceptance we've been given in Christ. Thus, Christians should be truly uncomfortable with their representatives using violence to achieve ends that are not to genuinely protect the innocent and punish evil. Because many occupational licensing laws also significantly harm many in lower income jobs,[82] Christians ought to worry that one who supports burdensome regulation "closes his ear to the cry of the poor" and "will himself call out and not be answered."[83]

WHY WE SHOULD STOP TRYING TO ELECT A SAVIOR

Considering everything that the market and a bevy of emerging, private institutions and charities can provide and the impact that those provisions have the potential to make, we see a different perspective on the social change that is possible. Rather than rely on candidates, political parties, and acts of government, we have an opportunity to remember that Christ's kingdom was not built upon political foundations. Instead, early Christianity was a movement that swept the world in spite of the edicts of kings. In some places in the world, it still is. The heroes that have lived and died for the gospel, served the poor, and fought for change have done so regardless of the parties in power and, in many cases, pushed against the tides of governments—democratic or otherwise.

If our ultimate hopes are in the hands of Christ, cradled in the spaces left by his scars, then we cannot lose. No circumstances or actions of humans, no matter how unpleasant they may be, can deprive us of our ultimate identities and a hope that transcends. Consequently, we are freed from distraction by the actions of governments and politicians. They will always exist and will never be able to save us from want, old age, sickness, or uncertainty. That won't stop governments or politicians from promising it. And when they do promise the impossible, as Jason's chapter reminds us, we must resist the temptation to "trust in princes," who cannot save.[84]

---

81. Matt 5:9

82. De Rugy. "Occupational Licensing: Bad for Competition, Bad for Low-Income Workers."

83. Prov 21:13

84. Ps 146:3

This is a call to faith but not in governments or in any other human institutions. Of all the human institutions that compete for our idolatrous attention, government most frequently wins. Here in America, it wins most often due to the cultural reverence for the founding era and the widespread Christianity of that time. Viewing the American experiment as somehow holy, or a major part in God's plan for mankind, there is a temptation among American Christians to bind up their national and eternal identities. More than that, there is also an American sentiment of wanting to look backward or to return to a time when the founding ideas still prevailed. What we miss, when we focus too heavily on a moment that has passed, is what we could be discovering, just around the next bend, which may be even better than what we had before. This is why the call to be a bard for optimism is so necessary—because the future needs an advocate.

If you actually study the writings of the Founding Fathers, they were heralds for a new nation, a new way of looking at government which, for the first time in history, would operate without a king, without an emperor, or without anyone else ruling by a so-called divine right. For that vision, shaped by a profound respect for their historical rights as Englishmen, they were willing to pledge their lives and their sacred honors. And this is a balance libertarian Christians can strike, in a way that slightly and respectfully differs from conservative Christians. We can appreciate the past, as did the founders, and keep alive the traditions and arrangements which have succeeded in carrying us through to the present. However, we must continue the process of spontaneous order, of discovery, and take that legacy forward to defend essential principles and their enduring value, not just their ties to a golden age we idealize in memory. Rather than making our founders or our heroes into idols, let's make them the bards with breadcrumbs and follow their lead.

Beyond romanticizing "ideal" political leaders or thinkers, trust in the political systems around us also fosters a disconnect. As Frederic Bastiat's writings point out, there is a contradiction in any ideology that simultaneously believes that men are depraved and not worthy of self-direction yet believes that "the tendencies of organizers are always good."[85] If our representatives and leadership are taken from the same common stock of humanity of which you and I are a part, then why do we assume that their elections will make them more pure?

85. Bastiat, *The Law*, 46.

By giving them access to more power, more control, more entitlement, and less consequence, why would we believe that this would be edifying? As Bastiat's argument continues, we would have to believe that politicians "are made of a finer clay than the rest of mankind [. . .] and the organizers have received from Heaven an intelligence and virtue that place them beyond and above mankind."[86] As later thinkers, beginning with James Buchanan and Gordon Tullock, elaborated in what has become the public choice perspective, this view looks at politics through rose-colored glasses.[87] In reality, the public choice school teaches us that politicians, just like the rest of us, respond to incentives. Also like the rest of us, they participate in politics as they would in any other marketplace. They seek to advantage themselves first and foremost, because the system around them offers them perks and benefits that are nearly irresistible.

Thus, we shouldn't be surprised when politicians inevitably disappoint us. When they don't fulfill a promise, when their term ends, when we're not all blissfully happy and free of all that ails us, and when the streets aren't paved with a gold that never succumbs to potholes and bad drivers, none of this should be startling. Humans were never intended to be gods, and this world was never meant to be heaven. Thus, human government can't take us there. Yet neither can even a perfectly unregulated free market economy, brimming with entrepreneurial possibility.

What I defend is not a counterutopia but rather a vision for minimizing, in our view, the role of government so that we can focus on attempting to provide, through more effective and empowering means, for the needs of the real people we see on a daily basis. While this won't be perfect, won't pave our streets in gold, and won't solve all the ills of uncertainty and old age, it will help us to serve our neighbors in realistic and small ways. And if, from the start, we don't idealize or idolize what's possible, then we will be grateful for the small improvements.

Thus, the libertarian Christian's way of approaching government and social institutions in general should be to avoid the idolatry of control that, through the fears inherent in a life on earth, tempts us to place trust where it doesn't belong. By heightening our tolerance for risk and our trust in each other, we can solve more problems, using our energy to attack them ourselves instead of waiting for people who hundreds of miles away and who often believe themselves to be of different clay to solve them for us.

86. Ibid.
87. Buchanan, *Public Choice*, 11.

SO WHAT'S NEXT?

After a thorough consideration of the sources of hope and solutions that are available to us and the dangers of misplacing our hopes and optimism, it's now time to apply those considerations to the life we will live. If libertarian Christians take seriously the callings of the great commission[88] and of our mandate to fill and subdue the earth,[89] we should take stock of the problems around us and determine which may be within our powers to solve. Beyond that, we should also fill our minds and our lives with sources of information that challenge us, educate us, and share with us a small fraction of the knowledge that's out there, telling us a different story—that things are getting a lot better for a lot of people. Considering we've been given this earth to subdue to glorify God and to serve our fellow men, that's good news. It isn't *the* good news, but it's a foreshadowing of the redemption to come and all that Christ promises to accomplish for those who place into his hands their lives, their sacred honors, and their eternal hopes.

88. Matt 28:19–20
89. Gen 1:28

BIBLIOGRAPHY

"About Us," Enabling The Future, accessed July 10, 2016, http://enablingthefuture.org/about/.

Addady, Michael. "Sheetz Is About to Make Its Employees Very Happy." *Fortune,* January 12, 2016. http://fortune.com/2016/01/12/sheetz-raises-employee-wages/.

Allen, Curtis. "Daniel 3: Realistic Faith." Sermon, Redeemer Church of Arlington, Arlington, VA, September 15, 2013. http://redeemerarlington.com/speakers /curtis-allen/

Bailey, Ronald. "The Decline of Violence." *Reason.com,* February, 2012. https://reason.com/archives/2012/01/11/the-decline-of-violence.

Bastiat, Frederic. *The Law.* Auburn: The Mises Institute, 2007.

Block, Walter. "Libertarianism vs. Libertinism." *The Journal of Libertarian Studies* 11 (1994): 117. https://mises.org/library/libertarianism-and-libertinism.

Buchanan, James. *Public Choice: The Origins and Development of a Research Program,* 2003. https://www.gmu.edu/centers/publicchoice/pdf%20links/Booklet.pdf.

Carey, Jesse. "Why You Should Be Optimistic About The Future." *Relevant,* December 29, 2015. http://www.relevantmagazine.com/current/why-you-should-be-optimistic-about-future.

Carter, Stephen L. "Law Puts Us All In Same Danger as Eric Garner," *Bloomberg,* December 4, 2014. http://www.bloomberg.com/view/articles/2014-12-04/law-puts-us-all-in-same-danger-as-eric-garner.

Crews, Clyde Wayne. "Ten Thousand Commandments 2015." *Competitive Enterprise Institute,* May 8, 2015. https://cei.org/10kc2015.

De Rugy, Veronique. "Occupational Licensing: Bad for Competition, Bad for Low-Income Workers," *Mercatus Center at George Mason University,* March 25, 2014. http://mercatus.org/publication/occupational-licensing-bad-competition-bad-low-income-workers.

The Economist. "The $1-a-Week School." August 1, 2015. http://www.economist.com/news /leaders/21660113-private-schools-are-booming-poor-countries-governments-should-either-help-them-or-get-out.

"Fast Facts," National Center for Education Statistics, accessed July 10, 2016, http://nces.ed.gov/fastfacts/display.asp?id=84.

Folsom, Burton W. *The Myth of the Robber Barons.* 4th ed. Herndon: Young America's Foundation, 2003.

Food And Agriculture Organization of the United Nations. *The State of Food Insecurity in the World 2015.* Rome: FAO. 2015. http://www.fao.org/3/a-i4646e/i4646e01.pdf.

GBD 2013 Mortality and Causes of Death Collaborators. "Global, Regional, and National Age-Sex Specific All-Cause and Cause-Specific Morality for 240 Causes of Death, 1990–2013," *The Lancet* 385, no. 9963 (2003): 117–171, doi: http://dx.doi.org/10.1016/S0140-6736(14)61682-2.

Grudem, Wayne. *Politics According to the Bible: A Comprehensive Resource for Understanding Modern Political Issues in Light of Scripture.* Grand Rapids, MI: Zondervan, 2010.

Hayek, F.A. *The Fatal Conceit: The Errors of Socialism.* Chicago: The University of Chicago Press, 1988.

Hayek, F.A. "The Use of Knowledge in Society." *American Economic Review* XXXV, no. 4 (1945): 519–30. http://www.econlib.org/library/Essays/hykKnw1.html.

The Hobbit: An Unexpected Journey. Directed by Peter Jackson. 2012. Burbank, CA & Beverly Hills, CA: Warner Bros. Entertainment Inc. and Metro-Goldwyn-Mayer Productions, 2012. DVD.

Huemer, Michael. *The Problem of Political Authority: An Examination of the Right to Coerce and the Duty to Obey.* New York: Palgrave Macmillan, 2013.

Jacobellis v. Ohio, 378 US 184 (1964).

Lewis, C.S. *The Weight of Glory: And Other Addresses.* New York: Harper One, 2001.

Malcolm, John. "Criminal Law and the Administrative State: The Problem with Criminal Regulations." *Legal Memorandum #130 on Legal Issues,* August 6, 2014. http://www.heritage.org/research/reports/2014/08/criminal-law-and-the-administrative-state-the-problem-with-criminal-regulations#_ftn8.

McCloskey, Deidre N. *Bourgeois Dignity: Why Economics Can't Explain The Modern World.* Chicago and London: The University of Chicago Press, 2010.

Morgan, Edmund S. "Puritan Hostility to the Theater." *Proceedings of the American Philosophical Society* 110, no. 5 (1966): 340–347. https://www.jstor.org/stable/986023?seq=2#page_scan_tab_contents.

Noell, Edd S., Stephen L.S. Smith, and Bruce G. Webb. *Economic Growth: Unleashing the Potential of Human Flourishing.* Washington, DC: AEI, 2013.

Perry, Mark J. "Chart of the greatest and most remarkable achievement in human history, thanks to free market capitalism." *AEI Ideas* (blog), July 13, 2015. https://www.aei.org/publication/chart-of-the-greatest-and-most-remarkable-achievement-in-human-history-thanks-to-free-market-capitalism/.

Pinter, Steven. "Violence Vanquished." *The Wall Street Journal,* September 4, 2011. http://www.wsj.com/articles/SB10001424053111904106704576583203589408180.

Postrel, Virginia. *The Future And Its Enemies: The Growing Conflict Over Creativity, Enterprise, and Progress.* New York: Touchstone, 1998.

Rand, Ayn. *Atlas Shrugged.* New York: Signet, 1996.

"Reg Stats." *Regulatory Studies Center.* https://regulatorystudies.columbian.gwu.edu/reg-stats#Total%20Pages%20in%20the%20Code%20of%20Federal%20Regulations%20%281936%20-%202013%29.

Roosevelt, Franklin D: "State of The Union Message to Congress," January 11, 1944, transcript, Franklin D. Roosevelt Presidential Library, http://www.fdrlibrary.marist.edu/archives/address_text.html.

Shaver, Andrew. "You're More Likely To Be Fatally Crushed By Furniture Than Killed By A Terrorist." *The Washington Post,* November 23, 2015. https://www.washingtonpost.com/news/monkey-cage/wp/2015/11/23/youre-more-likely-to-be-fatally-crushed-by-furniture-than-killed-by-a-terrorist/.

Smith, Adam. *The Wealth of Nations.* New York: Bantom Dell, 2003.

Smith, Kyle. "The Greatest Food in Human History." *New York Post,* July 28, 2013. http://nypost.com/2013/07/28/the-greatest-food-in-human-history/.

Walsh, Brian J. and J. Richard Middleton. *The Transforming Vision: Shaping a Christian Worldview.* Downers Grove, IL: InterVarsity, 1984.

Wolters, Albert M. *Creation Regained: Biblical Basics for a Reformational Worldview.* Grand Rapids, MI: Wm. B. Eerdmans, 2005.

World Bank. *Electric Power Consumption,* 2014, http://data.worldbank.org/indicator/EG.USE.ELEC.KH.PC.

5

The State is No Savior

Philip Luca

I was four when the Iron Curtain fell. That same year, my uncle brought me on a tour around the flour mill where he worked. Trains hauled in tons of wheat. Giant machines ground the wheat into flour. At the end of the production line, my eyes grew when I saw what was baking inside the oversized ovens: pretzel sticks—one of my favorite foods.

As we prepared to leave, my uncle looked both ways before snatching a loaf of bread from the conveyer belt. That was what we ate for dinner that night and for lunch the next day.

I was six when I first learned about the Ten Commandments in Sunday school. One commandment in particular stuck in my mind after class: "Thou shalt not steal." I thought back to the day my uncle took a loaf of bread from the mill. Knowing my uncle was a godly man, I asked him why he broke one of God's commandments. He looked at me with sorrowed eyes and said, "I did what I had to do."

His answer only raised more questions for me. *Why wasn't there enough bread for everyone? What would happen if we didn't have any bread?*

I hope you are never faced with the difficult decision of whether or not to steal in order to provide for your family. In Romania, where I grew up, many people felt they did not have the choice. Sometimes it was necessary for survival.

The food shortage of my childhood was born from decades of collective agriculture and state-run farming. Our iron-fisted leader, Nicolae Ceaușescu, forced food price ceilings and the export of a majority of our agricultural products to repay our nation's debt. Strict food rations on bread, milk, butter, eggs, sugar, and meat followed. My grandfather waited in line for hours at a time just to buy one gallon of milk—the only ration he was allowed each week. It was common practice for mill workers to steal flour or bread from their workplace and trade it for other groceries on the black market.

Frequent blackouts accompanied food shortages. Sometimes these blackouts lasted two days at a time. Energy rations on electricity, heating, air conditioning, and even television became a way of life. The government restricted TV broadcasting to two hours each day with access to only one channel. Much of that time was filled with Soviet propaganda describing the false "accomplishments" of the Romanian economy.

I wish this wasn't my story. I wish this wasn't the story of my family and friends and millions of people across the globe. I am thankful for the opportunity to have moved with my family to the United States in 2005. I consider myself one of the lucky ones. Sadly, though, too many people around the world do not have the chance to live in a free society.

Approximately 94 million people died from the atrocities of communism in the twentieth century. That's more than the death count of homicide (58 million) and genocide (30 million) combined.[1] This deadly social experiment, born in ivory towers, spread throughout Eastern Europe in the twentieth century. It lingers in many parts of the world today, most fatally in North Korea where some consider modern humanitarian crimes comparable to what the Nazis did in the Second World War.[2]

Why would anyone want to give up such freedom to begin with? Perhaps the desire for an all-powerful government comes from the same human desire the Israelites expressed in First Samuel 8 when they begged Samuel for a king. At their very core, all people want to be led. All people want a hero, a savior.

Maybe the Romanians who supported communism looked desperately to the government as their savior. Perhaps regime leaders believed they were all-powerful, capable of providing for everyone according to their needs. Their pride ignored all laws of human nature and economic reality, so the devastation of an entire nation was less than surprising.

Winston Churchill said, "Socialism is a philosophy of failure, the creed of ignorance, and the gospel of envy, its inherent virtue is the equal sharing

1. Quick, "20th Century Death."
2. Nebehay, "North Korea Crimes Evoke Nazi Era."

of misery."[3] Churchill was right. The only thing anyone ever received from the communist state was an equal share of misery and poverty.

Not only did the communist government deprive us of a flourishing life and our own human dignity, but they actively attempted to silence Christianity. It was common for Christians to receive fines from the state or lose their government jobs for living a life of faith. My grandfather lost two months' salary for holding prayer in his workplace. My father refused to turn over his Bible while in the army, so the government sentenced him to a labor camp. One of Romania's most well-known evangelical pastors, Joseph Ton, was exiled for spreading "propaganda which endangers the security of the state."[4]

It is possible the rulers saw faith as a threat to their own authority—Christians answer to an authority higher than that of the Romanian government. To Romania's regime, there was no room for any savior other than itself.

Whispers of the salvific power of government are infused in modern social justice ideology. Many progressives want the government to play a larger role in forcibly redistributing wealth, regulating private enterprise, and providing welfare entitlements. A 2011 Rasmussen poll shows 11 percent of Americans believe communism would better serve this country's needs than our current system.[5] Too many still hope the government will do the one thing it most certainly cannot do: save us.

Christ addresses both physical poverty and spiritual poverty in the Bible. The state cannot properly address either. In the fullest expression of charity, Christ gives of himself freely to us. Yet, even the most benevolent national leader is incapable of addressing the poverty of a single individual without first taking from another. In this material transfer, there is no charity. There is only force.

I lived under a state that desperately wanted to be a savior and imploded under the weight of its own pride. Ceaușescu was tried and executed on Christmas Day, 1989, during the Romanian Revolution. Through much needed government reform,[6] Romanians continue to pick up the pieces of

3. Krieg, *The New American Newspeak Dictionary*, 96.

4. Nichols, "Once-Exiled Cleric A Hero."

5. Ramussen Report. "11% Say Communism Better Than U.S. System of Politics." March 15, 2011.

6. "Romania."

their broken society. Yet some still yearn for the restoration of the communist regime.[7]

As a people called to freedom, let us not forget the horror we beg for when we make the state our savior from life's problems. When we ask the government for prosperity, we receive poverty. When we ask the government for charity, we receive plunder. When we ask the government for progress, we receive regressions. When we ask the government for life, we receive deathly burdens. While certain functions of government may be right and just, the state is fundamentally incapable of prescribing morality, giving life meaning, or saving us from the grip of sin.

In John 6:35, Christ calls himself "the bread of life" and says whoever comes to him will not hunger.[8] He is the compass that directs our path. Even under the threat of a power-hungry state, Christ remains. His body and blood give us life. *He* is Savior.

Christ did not rescue us from sin to give us more stuff on earth. He rescued us so that we can *be* more on earth—more loving, more just, more human. He met us physically in the world to heal broken bodies, feed the hungry, and make the blind see. His earthly miracles all point to the heavenly, the eternal—the mending of our souls. Under any form of government of which we might live, Christ heals us so we can participate in the divine life here and now.

How, then, can we exemplify hope in a world that sometimes seems so hopeless? Remembering Gandalf's words in the film *The Hobbit*, as Leah Hughey mentions in the previous chapter, "it is the small things, everyday deeds of ordinary folk that keeps the darkness at bay. Simple acts of kindness and love."[9]

At the age of eight, while I was still living in Romania, a young boy and girl knocked on our front door. They appeared homeless and the boy looked about my age. They said they were hungry and asked if we had any food to spare. Even at my age I wondered, *why don't they have a home and parents to feed them like I do?*

My mom asked me and my siblings to cook a meal for them. We dug through our fridge and threw together a humble smorgasbord. As we sat down to eat together, I imagined myself in the boy's shoes. He said, "Thank you," and smiled at me before reaching for the bread.

7. Odobescu, "Struggling Romanians Yearn for Communism."
8. John 6:35
9. *The Hobbit*, Scene 20, directed by Peter Jackson.

In that moment, it wasn't the "great power" of the Romanian regime that provided a meal and a little compassion to the destitute and lonely children at my door. It was, as Tolkien says, "small acts of kindness and love" from one fellow citizen to another. Embedded deeply in the freedom to serve passionately, act bravely, and love fiercely, there is a hope that cannot be shaken by any man. For Christ himself tells us that if the Son has set us free, we will be free indeed.[10]

No matter how small they may appear, I hold fast to these little moments of freedom. Even under the shadow of force, destitution, and captivity, we are all called to make tiny dents in the darkness. We are called to be free.

10. John 8:36

BIBLIOGRAPHY

The Hobbit: An Unexpected Journey. Directed by Peter Jackson. 2012. Burbank, CA & Beverly Hills, CA: Warner Bros. Entertainment Inc. and Metro-Goldwyn-Mayer Productions, 2012. DVD.Krieg, Adrian H. *The New American Newspeak Dictionary: Without Prejudice.* Bradenton, Florida: A2z, 2005.

Nebehay, Stephanie, and Tom Miles. "North Korea Crimes Evoke Nazi Era, Kim May Face Charges: U.N. Inquiry." *Reuters*, February 18, 2014. http://www.reuters.com/article/us-korea-north-un-inquiry-idUSBREA1H1HN20140218.

Nichols, Mike. "Once-Exiled Cleric A Hero In Romania." *Chicago Tribune*, January 19, 1990. http://articles.chicagotribune.com/1990-01-19/news/9001050862_1_dumitru-mazilu-nicolae-ceausescu-romanian-language.

Odobescu, Vlad. "Struggling Romanians Yearn for Communism." *The Washington Times*, August 20, 2012. http://www.washingtontimes.com/news/2012/aug/30/struggling-romanians-yearn-for-communism/.

Quick, Miriam. "20th Century Death." *Information Is Beautiful*, accessed August 3, 2016. http://www.informationisbeautiful.net/visualizations/20th-century-death/.

Ramussen Report. "11% Say Communism Better Than U.S. System of Politics." March 15, 2011. http://www.rasmussenreports.com/public_content/politics/general_politics/march_2011/11_say_communism_better_than_u_s_system_of_politics_and_economics.

"Romania: On the Way to Recovery through Prudent Macroeconomic Management." *The World Bank*, April 11, 2013. www.worldbank.org/en/results/2013/04/11/romania-on-the-way-to-recovery-through-prudent-macroeconomic-management.

Afterword
Elise Daniel

Imagine if, at the snap of your fingers, you had the power to instantly shrink the size of government. That would be great, wouldn't it? But, have you considered what a smaller government would require of you, especially as a Christian?

In *What's Wrong with the World*, G.K. Chesterton says, "Most modern freedom is at root fear. It is not so much that we are too bold to endure rules; it is rather that we are too timid to endure responsibilities."[1] A libertarian Christian cannot wish for a smaller government without the willingness to take up the burden of responsibility that comes with that freedom.

In a society with a smaller government, our faith must grow larger. Freedom requires *more* of us, not less. Libertarian Christians cannot simply sit around philosophizing about a better world. We must begin creating one now.

Lord Acton declared that freedom is not "the power of doing what we like, but the right of being able to do what we ought."[2] What would a free society be without the church fighting on the front lines of poverty relief? Or without the body of Christ leading creativity and innovation in our vocations? Or without Christians living lives of love and mercy?

Perhaps the libertarian libertine would claim accountability to only him- or herself, based on what they value subjectively as individuals. But much more is required for the libertarian Christian. We cannot consider

1. Chesterton, *What's Wrong With the World*, 254.
2. Ballor, *Lord Acton on Catholic and Modern Views of Liberty.*

141

political liberty without asking ourselves, *Am I ready to live a life that takes up the burden of a free society?*

The Christian faith should not only inspire hope for "the city that is to come,"[3] but also for freedom, justice, and mercy on earth *now*—and there is much to hope for.

One hour of the nightly news makes us well aware of the sin and suffering in the world: political corruption, global poverty, escalating unrest in the Middle East, and mass persecution of Christians around the world. The evils we see on a day-to-day basis, while alarming, should not cause us to fear. Jesus told his disciples, in light of all the things they would endure, to take heart because "I have overcome the world."[4] Rather, the sin in our broken society presents trillions of tiny opportunities to freely give of ourselves in reflection of Christ's love.

We often overwhelm ourselves when we talk about "ending poverty" and "fighting for social justice." We fail to wrap our minds around the complexity of the world's problems. Then, the devil on our shoulder whispers, "just don't do *anything.*" In those moments, we risk forgetting how God operates. He weaves his justice, mercy, and love into the mundaneness of our everyday lives.

You can begin taking up the burden of a free society right now, right where you are. For example, you can start by learning about the needs in your community—at church, work, school, or home—by building a relationship with an individual on the margins of society (and we are all on the margins sometimes).

Spend time with someone you wouldn't normally spend time with—someone different than you, someone who is disconnected from community, or someone who is suffering. Learn about their life and who they are. The next time someone pops in your head—whether it's a friend, family member, coworker, roommate, an acquaintance, or even someone you hardly know—consider if God is nudging you to pray for that person. Send him or her a text to see how their day is going. Ask them to lunch. Give a hug. Offer a ride to the grocery store.

When we bring those on the margins into community, they are known and their needs are known. When we know what someone needs spiritually, relationally, and physically, we have an opportunity to help meet his or her needs.

3. Heb 13:14
4. John 16:33

We are to love the world dearly, as followers of the one who arranged its every atom, the one who made mankind to bear his image. Yet, as residents in a fallen world, we desire something greater: that justice would be sought and mercy would be loved, that the chains of injustice would be loosed and the oppressed would be set free.[5]

We are called to use our freedom—spiritual freedom, political freedom, *all* freedoms—to love and serve one another. This is the mission of the libertarian Christian.

Are you willing to help carry the burden of an imperfect and free society?

> *For you were called to freedom, brothers. Only do not use your freedom as an opportunity for the flesh, but through love serve one another. For the whole law is fulfilled in one word: "You shall love your neighbor as yourself."*
>
> —Galatians 5:13–15

---

5. Isa 58:6

BIBLIOGRAPHY

Ballor, Jordan. "Lord Acton on Catholic and Modern Views of Liberty." *The Acton Institute*, July 17, 2013. http://blog.acton.org/archives/57615-lord-acton-on-catholic-and-modern-views-of-liberty.html

Chesterton, Gilbert K. *What's Wrong With the World*. New York: Dodd, Mead and Company, 1910.

Made in the USA
Las Vegas, NV
09 December 2023